# LOOKING FROM WITHIN

# LOOKING FROM WITHIN

## A Seeker's Guide to Attitudes for Mastery and Inner Growth

*Gleanings from the Works of*
SRI AUROBINDO
and
THE MOTHER

*Compiled with an Introduction by*
A. S. Dalal

SRI AUROBINDO ASHRAM
PONDICHERRY

First Edition: 1995
Reprinted: 1996, 1999, 2002

(Typeset in 10/12 New Times Roman)

Rs. 55.00
ISBN 81-7058-406-X

Published by Sri Aurobindo Ashram Publication Department,
Pondicherry - 605 002
Printed at Sri Aurobindo Ashram Press, Pondicherry
PRINTED IN INDIA

# CONTENTS

## SECTION I

### Looking at Life and Circumstances

## SECTION II

### Looking at Oneself and Others

The inner spiritual progress does not depend on outer conditions so much as in the way we react to them from within – that has always been the ultimate verdict of spiritual experience. It is why we insist on taking the right attitude and persisting in it, on an inner state not dependent on outer circumstances, a state of equality and calm, if it cannot be at once of inner happiness, on going more and more within and LOOKING FROM WITHIN* outwards instead of living in the surface mind which is always at the mercy of the shocks and blows of life. It is only from that inner state that one can be stronger than life and its disturbing forces and hope to conquer.

SRI AUROBINDO

(*Letters on Yoga*, Sri Aurobindo Birth Centenary Library, Vol. 23, pp. 650-51)

* Capital letters by the compiler.

# PREFACE

Three chief categories of seekers have been kept in view in selecting passages for this compilation: those who wish to obtain a greater life-mastery and self-mastery; those who, while pursuing the common goals of life, also aim at something beyond the ordinary life and seek to grow towards a higher or spiritual state of being; those for whom spiritual growth is the primary purpose and pre-occupation of life. The differences in interests and spiritual outlook of these three types of seekers account for the assorted nature of the contents of the book regarding the topics covered and the level of understanding called for.

All of the many approaches for the attainment of mastery and inner growth involve the cultivation of certain attitudes which, as explained in the Introduction to this book, are related to inner or psychological states from which we look at and react to everything in life, both within us and outside us. This book deals with such basic attitudes in the light of Sri Aurobindo's yoga.

In order that the book may have a wider appeal, the selection of passages included here has been limited to those which are apt to be meaningful not only to followers of Sri Aurobindo and the Mother but also to seekers outside this circle. Special terms and concepts pertaining to Sri Aurobindo's yoga with which the general reader may be unfamiliar have been explained in the Glossary at the end of the book.

Passages in this book have been derived from two main sources: letters of Sri Aurobindo to disciples, and talks by the Mother to the children of the Ashram. The nature of these sources accounts for the less formal style which characterises many of the passages.

The contents of the book have been classified into sections and subsections to facilitate understanding and reference. However, many passages could have been included in any of several sections – an overlapping which makes the classification arbitrary to some extent. Therefore, for purposes of reference, the reader may find the Index at the end of the book to be more useful than the table of contents.

A. S. DALAL

# INTRODUCTION

The essential difference between an animal and a human being, states Sri Aurobindo, is that the animal "cannot get for one moment away from its origins... and become something greater than its present self, a more free, magnificent and noble being",[1] whereas the human being has the potential ability to exceed and even transform the basic instinctive nature which he shares with the animal. Therefore, whereas the animal always remains an animal, man can grow into a being who is as much above the human being as the human being is above the animal.

This immense difference between man and animal is due to several distinguishing features of their psychological natures. First, consciousness in the human being has developed the power of detachment, that is, of standing back and observing things as a spectator.[2] Human consciousness can detach itself and stand back not only from what lies outside in the environment but also from internal thoughts and feelings, thus dividing itself into a part that observes and a part that is observed. This power of detachment makes for a *reflective* intelligence which a human

1. Sri Aurobindo, *The Synthesis of Yoga*, Sri Aurobindo Birth Centenary Library, Vol. 21 (Pondicherry. Sri Aurobindo Ashram), p. 598.

2. "It [consciousness] is not by its nature detached from the mental and other activities. It can be detached, it can be involved. In the human consciousness it is as a rule always involved, but it has developed the power of detaching itself – a thing which the lower creation seems unable to do. As the consciousness develops, this power of detachment also develops." – Sri Aurobindo, *Letters on Yoga*, Sri Aurobindo Birth Centenary Library, Vol. 23 (Pondicherry: Sri Aurobindo Ashram), p. 686.

being is capable of exercising as distinguished from the *reactive* intelligence of the animal. With the power of detachment and a reflective intelligence, the human being can control, modify and overcome the force of instincts and impulses, unlike the animal which cannot act contrary to its innate nature. Secondly, though all behaviour in the animal as well as in the human being is purposive, that is, directed towards the fulfilment of some purpose or goal, the human being, as distinguished from the animal, has the potential of conceiving and pursuing higher goals – moral, intellectual and aesthetic – beyond the basic ones related to physical and biological existence. Thirdly, the more highly developed human being, in contrast to the animal, is discontented with what he is, and feels an urge for growth towards what he conceives to be an ideal state of being. A fourth distinguishing human characteristic – and this brings us to the subject-matter of this book – is that the human mind, unlike that of the animal, can look at something and react to it from different perspectives. In other words, the human being can adopt different attitudes to the same thing, event or circumstance. The enormous significance of this human characteristic is implicit in a statement made by William James, one of the most celebrated psychologists: "The greatest discovery of my generation is that men can alter their lives by altering their attitudes of mind".

What is meant by "attitude"? The phrase "attitudes of mind" used by James obviously implies that attitudes have something to do with the mind. Thus dictionaries define attitude as "a way of thinking" or as "a mental view". A further understanding of the term is provided by psychology which defines attitude as an "internal affective orientation that would explain the actions of a person".[3] This psychological definition indicates that an attitude is not merely a way of thinking but also a way of feeling – an affective or emotional disposition – which determines a person's actions. In psychological jargon, an attitude has cognitive (thinking), affective (feeling) and conative (willing) components. Therefore, a change in one's attitude towards a thing, person, circumstance or event implies change in the way one thinks, feels and is disposed to act in relation to the thing, person, circumstance or event.[4]

The psychology of yoga throws further light on the nature of attitudes. Unlike modern psychology which lumps all psychological functions into what is called "mind", the psychology of yoga looks upon man's subjective nature as a composite of distinct though intermixed and interacting parts of the being, each with its own characteristic consciousness. This yoga concept of *parts of the being* is extremely helpful in understanding attitudes, because different attitudes are related to different parts of the being and their different types of consciousness. One's predominant attitudes depend on the part of the being which is dominant in one's nature. Broadly speaking, there are two divisions in the human being – the **outer being**, which constitutes the personality (from the Latin *persona*, "mask"), and the **inner being**, the true Being or

3. Arthur S. Reber, *The Penguin Dictionary of Psychology*, 1987, s.v. "attitude".

4. This point has been elaborated in "Attitudes, Mental Health and Yoga" in A.S. Dalal, *Psychology, Mental Health and Yoga*, (Pondicherry: Sri Aurobindo Ashram Press, and Ojai, California: Institute of Integral Psychology, 1991).

the Person who uses the outer mask of the personality.[5] The outer being is only an instrument as a means of expression; it is not one's real self. However, ordinarily we are identified with the outer being and regard it as our self. Therefore it is the outer being that usually expresses itself in our attitudes and actions.

The outer being is made up of three parts, each with its own distinct type of consciousness, distinguishable by its characteristic traits or qualities which are reflected in the attitudes pertaining to it. A description of these parts of the being is given below, using Sri Aurobindo's terminology.

**The physical (being):** Though people generally attribute consciousness and intelligence only to the mind, and look upon the body as something mechanical, the psychology of yoga reveals that the body is endowed with its own characteristic consciousness and intelligence. It is the consciousness in the body which regulates the complex workings of the different bodily organs and physiological systems. Though the mind exhibits a higher form of consciousness and intelligence than that of the body, it cannot but marvel at the wisdom of the body expressed in the various processes which maintain the body in health and heal it in illness or accident. However, physical consciousness, as compared to mental consciousness, is seen to be relatively inert, obscure, narrow or limited, and automatic or mechanical in its functionings. Thus attitudes which are characterised by rigidity, narrowness, conser-

5. In the Sankhya school of Indian philosophy, the outer and the inner divisions of the being are called Prakriti (Nature) and Purusha (Person) respectively.

vatism or slowness to change, indifference or boredom, and habitual or routine modes of action and reaction are related to the physical part of our being.

**The vital (being):** Intermediate between the physical and the mental is the vital, made up of life-energies, sensations (pleasure, pain, etc.), instincts and impulses (anger, fear, lust, etc.), desires, feelings and emotions. The vital (from the Latin word *vita*, "life"), is aptly so called because it is the source of life-force and seeks after life for its own sake, clinging to life even if it brings more of suffering than of pleasure. The vital consciousness is characterised by likes and dislikes, the search for pleasure and enjoyment, and the avoidance of pain and discomfort, desire to possess and to accumulate. Common attitudes based on the vital consciousness express a hedonistic orientation in life, what Freud referred to as "the pleasure principle". Besides the quest for pleasure these attitudes are characterised by a need for perpetual variety and change, ambitiousness, attachment and repulsion, aggression, fear and impulsiveness.

**The mental (being):** This is the part of our make-up which has to do with thoughts and ideas, facts and knowledge. Reason and intellect are the most highly developed expressions of the mental consciousness. In contrast to the vital which is governed by the pleasure principle, the mental is guided by what accords with reason and is deemed to be true or good. Therefore when the mental consciousness is predominant in an individual, the attitudes of the individual are characterised by a rational outlook and are based on moral and intellectual principles.

The differences among the parts of the outer being

described above are illustrated in Table 1 in relation to attitudes towards (1) life, (2) oneself and others, (3) work, and (4) difficulties.

It is interesting to note that the psychiatrist Karl Menninger, in describing the behaviour of human beings when faced with difficulties and obstacles in life, employs concepts which are analogous to the concepts of yoga psychology mentioned above. There are, says Menninger, five stages in man's response to life crises: Panic, Inertia, Striving, Coping, Mastery.[6] Panic, a characteristic of the vital consciousness, is often the first reaction to stress because in most human beings the vital is the predominant part of their nature. Inertia, which is the chief characteristic of the physical consciousness, may precede the stage of Panic as in the case of individuals who, dominated by the physical consciousness, lead a life of apathy until they are goaded by a dire difficulty which throws them into a state of panic. But the stage of Inertia often follows upon that of Panic when an individual, paralysed by an overwhelming difficulty, resigns himself to it or tries to escape from it. In terms of yoga psychology, such an individual, normally living predominantly in the vital consciousness, temporarily regresses as a result of stress to a state dominated by the physical consciousness. However, sooner or later, the majority of individuals recover at least to some extent from the initial reactions of panic and inertia, and learn to confront and combat their difficulties, thus entering the stage of Striving.

6. A further discussion of the subject will be found in "Mastery, Mental Health and Yoga" in A.S. Dalal, *Psychology, Mental Health and Yoga*.

## TABLE 1
## ATTITUDES OF THE OUTER BEING

| ATTITUDES TOWARDS | ATTITUDES OF THE PHYSICAL | ATTITUDES OF THE VITAL | ATTITUDES OF THE MENTAL |
|---|---|---|---|
| Life | Aimlessness; life governed by habit and routine. | Pursuit of wealth, sex and power; life governed by desire. | Pursuit of knowledge; life governed by moral and mental principles. |
| Oneself and Others* | Identification with the body. | Identification with impulses and emotions. | Identification with the mind. |
| Work | Chore; drudgery. | Means of earning, exercising power and exhibiting one's skills and abilities. | Performance of duty; rendering a service; means of self-expression and self-improvement. |
| Difficulties | Indifference; passive resignation; avoidance or escapism. | Struggle, anxiety and tension; irritability and aggression. | Dispassionate problem-solving. |

* The basic attitude towards oneself and others pertains to identificaton. All other attitudes stem from the nature of one's identification.

Note: Since all human beings have physical, vital and mental components in the make-up of their personality, the attitudes pertaining to these parts of the being exist in everybody. The attitudes vary in different persons in the degree of their predominance, depending on the extent to which each of the three parts of the being is dominant in a person.

In this stage, an individual, still living primarily in the vital consciousness, struggles against difficulties with the reactions of the vital consciousness, namely, instincts and impulses. But instinctive reactions, which serve the animal marvellously well in its struggle for existence, are inadequate guides for a human being because, in the first place, instincts in man are far inferior to those in the animal, and, secondly, because the problems which a human being has to tackle are far more complex than those faced by an animal, calling for an intelligence which can see beyond a limited sphere, where instincts are proverbially regarded as blind. Moreover, instincts in themselves pose a problem to the human being because of the perpetual conflicts between one instinct and another, and between instinct and reason. Thus, besides being inadequate for helping man in mastering the problems of life, instincts create an additional problem for the human being – the problem of self-mastery. Feelings and emotions, which, like instincts, also pertain to the vital consciousness, are indeed much more highly developed in the human being than even in the highest species of animal, but they have the same essential drawbacks as instincts: they operate within too narrow a sphere – primarily that of inter-personal relations – and, like instincts, they are fraught with conflict.

In the stage of Striving, during which human beings try to come to grips with the problems of life-mastery and self-mastery while still living predominantly in the vital consciousness, life is more or less a blind struggle, a groping towards ill-perceived and ever-eluding goals. The course of life is determined mostly by forces other than one's conscious choices and deliberate decisions. Therefore one's internal state is characterised by feelings of uncertainty, insecurity, conflict, anxiety and tension.

It is with the growth of the mental consciousness that one progressively learns to cope with the various internal and external stresses which every individual experiences in life. The stage of Coping, which is ushered in by the use of the power of reason and the exercise of mental will in the governance of life, is characterised by a certain sense of direction, inner ease, security and confidence.

Mastery, as conceived by Menninger, represents a further stage of psychological development when an individual no longer feels preyed upon by internal and external stresses, and meets the challenges of life with a clear sense of purpose, and with poise and serenity. From the viewpoint of yoga psychology, such a state of mastery pertains to a deeper consciousness than that of the outer being described previously. The deeper consciousness is that of the inner being, the Person within who is concealed by the outer being and whom we discover progressively with inner growth. Behind the physical, the vital and the mental parts of the outer being there is an inner or true physical, an inner or true vital and an inner or true mental which constitute our inner or true being. And behind both the outer and inner being is the innermost being, called by Sri Aurobindo the psychic, the individual soul, supporting the mental, vital, physical and psychic evolution of the being. Mastery, from the viewpoint of yoga psychology, begins when an individual, no longer completely identi-fied with the physical, vital and mental personality of the outer being, learns to live progressively in the deeper consciousness of the Person within. The attitudes of the inner consciousness from which such an individual looks at and reacts to everything in life are the subject-matter of this book. Cultivating these inner attitudes, which are partly illustrated in Table 2, is an effective means for growing into that deeper consciousness of freedom and mastery.

TABLE 2

INNER ATTITUDES

| Towards Life | Search for the purpose and meaning of life; pursuit of inner growth; life governed by what is felt to be the truth of one's inner being. |
| --- | --- |
| Towards Oneself and Others | Looking upon oneself and others as more than a physical-vital-mental being — as a Person. |
| Towards Work | A means of inner growth, self-offering and self-consecration. |
| Towards Difficulties | Viewing difficulties with equanimity, as opportunities for inner growth. |

A purely animal existence, governed by the vital consciousness, represents, in Menninger's terms, the stage of Striving, popularly described as the animal's struggle for existence. Though human beings are endowed with mental consciousness and have therefore learned to some extent to cope with the problems of life, most human beings are still primarily ruled by the vital consciousness, and therefore lead a life largely characterised by striving and struggling, very similar to that of the animal. But, unlike the animal, the human being, as previously stated, is a discontented creature, for he knows in the recesses of his inmost being that he has the power to free himself from the bonds of animal existence and become master of his destiny. As the Mother remarks:

> "... the vast majority of men are like prisoners with all the doors and windows closed, so they suffocate, which is quite natural. But they have with them the key that opens the doors and windows...."[7]

This book offers help for using the key.

A. S. DALAL

7. The Mother, *Questions and Answers 1957-58*, Collected Works of the Mother, Vol. 9 (Pondicherry: Sri Aurobindo Ashram), p. 431.

# I

# LOOKING AT LIFE AND CIRCUMSTANCES

# LOOKING AT LIFE AND CIRCUMSTANCES

## 1. Power of Attitude

Is it really the best that always happens?... It is clear that all that has happened had to happen: it could not be otherwise – by the universal determinism it had to happen. But we can say so only after it has happened, not before. For the problem of the very best that can happen is an individual problem, whether the individual be a nation or a single human being; and all depends upon the personal attitude. If, in the presence of circumstances that are about to take place, you can take the highest attitude possible – that is, if you put your consciousness in contact with the highest consciousness within reach, you can be absolutely sure that in that case it is the best that can happen to you. But as soon as you fall from this consciousness into a lower state, then it is evidently not the best that can happen, for the simple reason that you are not in your very best consciousness. I even go so far as to affirm that in the zone of immediate influence of each one, the right attitude not only has the power to turn every circumstance to advantage but can change the very circumstance itself. For instance, when a man comes to kill you, if you remain in the ordinary consciousness and get frightened out of your wits, he will most probably succeed in doing what he came for; if you rise a little higher and though full of fear call for the divine help, he may just miss you, doing you a slight injury; if, however, you have the right attitude and the full consciousness of the divine presence everywhere around you, he will not be able to lift even a finger against you....

I have had innumerable examples of the power of right attitude. I have seen crowds saved from catastrophes by one single person keeping the right attitude. But it must be an attitude that does not remain somewhere very high and leaves the body to its usual reactions. If you remain high up like that, saying, "Let God's will be done", you may get killed all the same. For your body may be quite undivine, shivering with fear: the thing is to hold the true consciousness in the body itself and not have the least fear and be full of the divine peace. Then indeed there is no danger. Not only can attacks of men be warded off, but beasts also and even the elements can be affected. I can give you a little example. You remember the night of the great cyclone, when there was a tremendous noise and splash of rain all about the place. I thought I would go to Sri Aurobindo's room and help him shut the windows. I just opened his door and found him sitting quietly at his desk, writing. There was such a solid peace in the room that nobody would have dreamed that a cyclone was raging outside. All the windows were wide open, not a drop of rain was coming inside.[1]

THE MOTHER

There is a state in which one realises that the effect of things, circumstances, all the movements and actions of life on the consciousness depends almost exclusively upon one's attitude to these things. There is a moment when one becomes sufficiently conscious to realise that things in themselves are truly neither good nor bad: they are this only in relation to us; their effect on us depends absolutely upon the attitude we have towards them. The same thing, identically the same, if we take it as a gift of God, as a divine grace, as the result of the full Harmony, helps us to become more conscious, stronger, more true, while if we take it – exactly the very same circumstance – as a blow from fate, as a bad force wanting to affect us, this constricts us, weighs us down and takes away from us all consciousness and strength and harmony. And the circumstance in itself is *exactly* the same – of this, I should like you all to have the experience, for when you have it, you become master of yourself. Not only master of yourself but, in what concerns you, master of the circumstances of your life. And this depends exclusively upon the attitude you take; it is not an experience that occurs in the head, though it begins there, but an experience which can occur in the body itself. So much so, that – well, it is a realisation which naturally asks for a lot of work, concentration, self-mastery, consciousness pushed into Matter, but as a result, in accordance with the way the body receives shocks from outside, the effect may be different. And if you attain perfection in that field, you become master of accidents. I hope this will happen. It is possible. It is not only possible, it is *certain*. Only it is just one step forward. That is, this power you have – already fully and formidably realised in the mind – to act upon circumstances to the extent of changing them totally in their action upon you, that power can descend into Matter, into the physical substance itself, the cells of the body, and give the same power to the body in relation to the things around it.

This is not a faith, it is a certitude that comes from experience.[2]

THE MOTHER

*There is no iron or ineffugable law that a given contact shall create pain or pleasure; it is the way the soul meets the rush or pressure of Brahman upon the members from outside them that determines either reaction.*

Sri Aurobindo
*Thoughts and Aphorisms*

It is obvious that the same event or the same contact causes pleasure in one and pain in another, depending on the inner attitude taken by each one.

And this observation leads towards a great realisation; for once one has not only understood but also felt that the Supreme Lord is the originator of all things and one remains constantly in contact with Him, all becomes the action of His Grace and is changed into calm and luminous bliss.[3]

THE MOTHER

## 2. The Determining Power is Within

You should not be so dependent on outward things; it is this attitude that makes you give so excessive an importance to circumstances. I do not say that circumstances cannot help or hinder – but they are circumstances, not the fundamental thing which is in ourselves, and their help or their hindrance ought not to be of primary importance. In yoga, as in every great or serious human effort, there is always bound to be an abundance of adverse interventions and unfavourable circumstances which have to be overcome. To give them too great an importance increases their importance and their power to multiply themselves, gives them, as it were, confidence in themselves and the habit of coming. To face them with equanimity – if one cannot manage a cheerful persistence against them of confident and resolute will – diminishes, on the contrary, their importance and effect and in the end, though not at once, gets rid of their persistence and recurrence. It is therefore a principle in yoga to recognise the determining power of what is within us – for that is the deeper truth – to set that right and establish the inward strength as against the power of outward circumstances. The strength is there – even in the weakest; one has to find it, to unveil it and to keep it in front throughout the journey and the battle.[4]

SRI AUROBINDO

In the play of the cosmic forces, the will in the cosmos – as one might say – does not always work apparently in favour of a smooth and direct line for the work or the sadhana; it often brings in what seem to be upheavals, sudden turns which break or deflect the line, opposing or upsetting circumstances or perplexing departures from what had been temporarily settled or established. The one thing is to preserve equanimity and make an opportunity and means of progress out of all that happens in the course of the life and the sadhana. There is a higher secret Will transcendent behind the play and will of the cosmic forces – a play which is always a mixture of things favourable and things adverse – and it is that Will which one must wait upon and have faith in; but you must not expect to be able always to understand its workings. The mind

wants this or that to be done, the line once taken to be
maintained, but what the mind wants is not at all always
what is intended in a larger purpose. One has to follow
indeed a fixed central aim in the sadhana and not deviate
from it, but not to build on outward circumstances,
conditions, etc., as if they were fundamental things.[5]

SRI AUROBINDO

... there are very many things one does and about which
one is not in the habit of thinking beforehand. When the
circumstance comes, one obeys it, so to say. And, indeed,
these things, like almost everything one does in life, are
not important in themselves. The only thing that matters
is the *attitude* with which they are done. The fact that you
do something because that action is present there before
you for one reason or another and that you are, so to say,
always obliged to act as long as you are in the outer
life – all this has a certain importance from the point of
view of the management of life if these acts are liable to
have far-reaching consequences in life, as for example,
getting married or going to live in one place or another or
taking up one occupation or another; these things are
generally considered important, and they are so to a
certain extent; but even for them, from the point of view
of yoga, everything depends much more on the attitude
one takes than on the thing itself. And so, above all, for
all the very small actions of daily life, the importance is
reduced to a minimum....

One may try to find out what is the truest thing to do,
but it is not by a mental discussion or a mental problem
that these things can be resolved. It is in fact by an inner

attitude which *creates* an atmosphere of harmony – progressive harmony – in which all one does will necessarily be the best thing that could be done in those particular circumstances. And the ideal would be an attitude complete enough for the action to be spontaneous, dictated by something other than an outer reason. But that is an ideal – for which one must aspire and which one can realise after some time. Till then, to take care always to keep the true attitude, the true aspiration, is much more important than to decide whether one will do gymnastic-marching or not and whether one will go to a certain class or not. Because these things have no real importance in themselves, they have only an altogether relative importance, the only important thing is just to keep the true orientation in one's aspiration and a living will for progress.[6]

THE MOTHER

## 3. The Right Spirit

*Aspire, concentrate in the right spirit and, whatever the difficulties, you are sure to attain the aim you have put before you.*

Sri Aurobindo
*Bases of Yoga*

*What is "the right spirit"?*

It depends on the case.... The right spirit is the will to perfect oneself, or the will to be calm, or... it depends, you see,... on the circumstances... it means that in each circumstance there is a spirit which is the suitable spirit, the one you ought to have, the attitude you must inwardly take. It depends on the case.

For example, you see, as soon as one feels a wave of physical disequilibrium, of ill health coming, well, to concentrate in the right spirit is to concentrate in an inner calm, a trust in the divine Grace, and a will to remain in physical equilibrium and good health. This is the right spirit. In another case, one may feel a wave of anger or a fit of temper coming from outside; then one should withdraw into an inner calm, a detachment from superficial things, with a will to express only what comes from above and always be submissive to the divine Will. This is the right spirit. And in each case it is something like that. Naturally it always comes back to the same thing, that one must remember the Divine and put oneself at His service and will what He wills.

But in one case you may want the calm, in the other you may want the force, in another still you may want health, in yet another something which resists the pressure from outside.

When one is perplexed, when one has to make a choice, when one doesn't know what the right thing to do is – you see, one has to choose among two or three or four possible decisions and doesn't know which is the right one, then one must put himself as far as possible in contact with his psychic being and the divine Presence in him, present the problem to this psychic consciousness and ask for the true light, the true decision, the one most in accordance with the divine Will, and try to listen and receive the inspiration.

In each case, you see, it is the right attitude.[7]

THE MOTHER

## 4. Seeking to Know

You must have a great deal of sincerity, a little courage and perseverance and then a sort of mental curiosity, you understand, curious, seeking to know, interested, wanting to learn. To love to learn: that, one must have in one's nature. Not to be able to bear standing before something grey, all hazy, in which nothing is seen clearly and which gives you quite an unpleasant feeling, for you do not know where you begin and where you end, what is yours and what is not yours and what is settled and what is not settled – what is this pulp-like thing you call yourself in which things get intermingled and act upon one another without even your being aware of it? You ask yourself: "But why have I done this?" You know nothing about it. "And why have I felt that?" You don't know that, either. And then, you are thrown into a world outside that is only fog and you are thrown into a world inside that is also for you another kind of fog, still more impenetrable, in which you live, like a cork thrown upon the waters and the waves carry it away or cast it into the air, and it drops and rolls on. That is quite an unpleasant state. I do not know, but to me it appears unpleasant.

To see clearly, to see one's way, where one is going, why one is going there, how one is to go there and what one is going to do and what is the kind of relation with others... But that is a problem so wonderfully interesting – it is interesting – and you can always discover things every minute! You can never have finished your work.

There is a time, there is a certain state of consciousness when you have the feeling that you are in that condition with all the weight of the world lying heavy upon you and

besides you are going in blinkers and do not know where
you are going, but there is something which is pushing
you. And that is truly a very unpleasant condition. And
there is another moment when one draws oneself up and is
able to see what is there above, and one becomes it; then
one looks at the world as though from the top of a very
very high mountain and one sees all that is happening
below; then one can choose one's way and follow it. That
is a more pleasant condition. This then is truly the truth,
you are upon earth *for that*, surely. All individual beings
and all the little concentrations of consciousness were
created to do this work. It is the very reson for existence:
to be able to become fully conscious of a certain sum of
vibrations representing an individual being and put order
therein and find one's way and follow the way.[8]

THE MOTHER

... when one wants to understand the deep laws of life,
wants to be ready to receive whatever message is sent by
the Divine, if one wants to be able to penetrate the secrets
of the Manifestation,... everything, no matter what, the
least little circumstance in life, becomes a teacher who can
teach you something, teach you how to think and act.
Even... the reflections of an ignorant child can help you to
understand something you didn't understand before.
Your attitude is so different. It is always an attitude which
is awaiting a discovery, an opportunity for progress, a
rectification of a wrong movement, a step ahead, and so it
is like a magnet that attracts from all around you oppor-
tunities to make this progress. The least things can teach
you how to progress. As you have the consciousness and

will to progress, everything becomes an opportunity, and you project this consciousness and will to progress upon all things.

And not only is this useful for you, but it is useful for all those around you with whom you have a contact.[9]

THE MOTHER

## 5. Listening to the Inner Law

The inner law, the truth of the being is the divine Presence in every human being, which should be the master and guide of our life.

When you acquire the habit of listening to this inner law, when you obey it, follow it, try more and more to let it guide your life, you create around you an atmosphere of truth and peace and harmony which naturally reacts upon circumstances and forms, so to say, the atmosphere in which you live. When you are a being of justice, truth, harmony, compassion, understanding, of perfect good-will, this inner attitude, the more sincere and total it is, the more it reacts upon the external circumstances; not that it necessarily diminishes the difficulties of life, but it gives these difficulties a new meaning and that allows you to face them with a new strength and a new wisdom; whereas the man, the human being who follows his impulses, who obeys his desires, who has no time for scruples, who comes to live in complete cynicism, not caring for the effect that his life has upon others or for the more or less harmful consequences of his acts, creates for himself an atmosphere of ugliness, selfishness, conflict and bad will which necessarily acts more and more upon his consciousness and gives a bitterness to his life that in the end becomes a perpetual torment.[10]

THE MOTHER

## 6. The Ordinary View of Spiritual Life

Throughout this teaching [of the Dhammapada] there is one thing to be noticed; it is this: you are never told that to live well, to think well, is the result of a struggle or of a sacrifice; on the contrary it is a delightful state which cures all suffering. At that time, the time of the Buddha, to live a spiritual life was a joy, a beatitude, the happiest state, which freed you from all the troubles of the world, all the sufferings, all the cares, making you happy, satisfied, contented.

It is the materialism of modern times that has turned spiritual effort into a hard struggle and a sacrifice, a painful renunciation of all the so-called joys of life.

This insistence on the exclusive reality of the physical world, of physical pleasures, physical joys, physical possessions, is the result of the whole materialistic tendency of human civilisation. It was unthinkable in ancient times. On the contrary, withdrawal, concentration, liberation from all material cares, consecration to the spiritual joy, that was happiness indeed.

From this point of view it is quite evident that humanity is far from having progressed; and those who were born into the world in the centres of materialistic civilisation have in their subconscient this horrible notion that only material realities are real and that to be concerned with things that are not material represents a wonderful spirit of sacrifice, an almost sublime effort. Not to be preoccupied from dawn to dusk and from dusk to dawn with all the little physical satisfactions, physical pleasures, physical sensations, physical preoccupations, is to bear evidence of a remarkable spirit. One is not aware of it, but the whole of modern civilisation is built on this conception: "Ah, what you can touch, you are sure that is true; what you can see, you are sure that is true; what you have eaten, you are sure of having eaten it; but all the rest – pooh! We are not sure whether they are not vain dreams and whether we are not giving up the real for the unreal, the substance for the shadow. After all, what are you going to gain? A few dreams! But when you have some coins in your pocket, you are sure that they are there!"

And that is everywhere, underneath everything. Scratch the appearances just a little, it is there, within your consciousness; and from time to time you hear this thing whispering within you, "Take care, don't be taken in." Indeed, it is lamentable.

We have been told that evolution is progressive and that it follows a spiral of ascending progression. I do not doubt that what one calls comfort in modern cities is a much higher degree of evolution than the comfort of the caveman. But in ancient narratives, they always spoke of a power of foresight, of the prophetic spirit, the announcement of future events through visions, life's intimacy with something more subtle that had for the simple people of that age a more concrete reality.

Now, in those beautiful cities that are so comfortable, when one wants to condemn anything, what does one say? – "It's a dream, it is imagination."

And precisely, if a person lives in an inner perception,

people look at him slightly askance and wonder whether he is altogether mentally sound. One who does not pass his time in striving for wealth or in trying to increase his comforts and well-being, to secure a good position and become an important person, a man who is not like that is mistrusted, people wonder whether he is in his right mind.

And all that is so much the stuff of the atmosphere, the content of the air you breathe, the orientation of the thoughts received from others that it seems absolutely natural. You do not feel that it is a grotesque monstrosity.

To become a little more conscious of oneself, to enter into relation with the life behind the appearances, does not seem to you to be the greatest good. When you sit in a comfortable chair, in front of a lavish meal, when you fill your stomach with delicious dishes, that certainly appears to you much more concrete and much more interesting. And if you look at the day that has passed, if you take stock of your day, if you have had some material advantage, some pleasure, a physical satisfaction, you mark it as a good day; but if you have received a good lesson from life, if it has given you a knock on your nose to tell you that you are a stupid fellow, you do not give thanks to the Grace, you say, "Oh, life is not always fun!"

When I read these ancient texts, I really have the impression that from the inner point of view, from the point of view of the true life, we have fallen back terribly and that for the acquisition of a few ingenious mechanisms, a few encouragements to physical laziness, the acquisition of instruments and gadgets that lessen the effort of living, we have renounced the reality of the inner life. It is that sense which has been lost and it needs an effort for you to think of learning the meaning of life, the purpose of existence, the goal towards which we must advance, towards which all life advances, whether you want it or not. One step towards the goal, oh! it needs so much effort to do that. And generally one thinks of it only when the outer circumstances are not pleasant.

How far we are from the times when the shepherd, who did not go to school and kept watch over his flock at night under the stars, could read in the stars what was going to happen, commune with something which expressed itself through Nature, and had the sense of the profound beauty and that peace which a simple life gives!

It is very unfortunate that one has to give up one thing in order to gain another. When I speak of the inner life, I am far from opposing any modern inventions, far from it, but how much these inventions have made us artificial and stupid! How much we have lost the sense of true beauty, how much we burden ourselves with useless needs!

Perhaps the time has come to continue the ascent in the curve of the spiral and now with all that this knowledge of matter has brought us, we shall be able to give to our spiritual progress a more solid basis. Strong with what we have learnt of the secrets of material Nature, we shall be able to join the two extremes and rediscover the supreme Reality in the very heart of the atom.[11]

THE MOTHER

## 7. The Spiritual View of the Ordinary Life

*"A principle of dark and dull inertia is at its [life's] base; all are tied down by the body and its needs and desires to a trivial mind, petty desires and emotions,*

*an insignificant repetition of small worthless function-*
*ings, needs, cares, occupations, pains, pleasures that*
*lead to nothing beyond themselves and bear the stamp*
*of an ignorance that knows not its own why and*
*whither. This physical mind of inertia believes in no*
*divinity other than its small earth-gods; it aspires*
*perhaps to a greater comfort, order, pleasure, but*
*asks for no uplifting and no spiritual deliverance. At*
*the centre we meet a stronger Will of life with a greater*
*gusto, but it is a blinded Daemon, a perverted spirit*
*and exults in the very elements that make of life a*
*striving turmoil and an unhappy imbroglio. It is a*
*soul of human or Titanic desire clinging to the garish*
*colour, disordered poetry, violent tragedy or stirring*
*melodrama of the mixed flux of good and evil, joy*
*and sorrow, light and darkness, heady rapture and*
*bitter torture. It loves these things and would have*
*more and more of them or, even when it suffers and*
*cries out against them, can accept or joy in nothing*
*else; it hates and revolts against higher things and in*
*its fury would trample, tear or crucify any diviner*
*Power that has the presumption to offer to make life*
*pure, luminous and happy and snatch from its lips the*
*fiery brew of that exciting mixture. Another Will-in-*
*Life there is that is ready to follow the ameliorating*
*ideal Mind and is allured by its offer to extract some*
*harmony, beauty, light, nobler order out of life, but*
*this is a smaller part of the vital nature and can be*
*easily overpowered by its more violent or darker*
*duller yoke-comrades; nor does it readily lend itself to*
*a call higher than that of the Mind unless that call*
*defeats itself, as Religion usually does, by lowering its*

*demand to conditions more intelligible to our obscure vital nature. All these forces the spiritual seeker grows aware of in himself and finds all around him and has to struggle and combat incessantly to be rid of their grip and dislodge the long-entrenched mastery they have exercised over his own being as over the environing human existence. The difficulty is great; for their hold is so strong, so apparently invincible that it justifies the disdainful dictum which compares human nature to a dog's tail, – for, straighten it never so much by force of ethics, religion, reason or any other redemptive effort, it returns in the end always to the crooked curl of Nature. And so great is the vim, the clutch of that more agitated Life-Will, so immense the peril of its passions and errors, so subtly insistent or persistently invasive, so obstinate up to the very gates of Heaven the fury of its attack or the tedious obstruction of its obstacles that even the saint and the Yogin cannot be sure of their liberated purity or their trained self-mastery against its intrigue or its violence."*

Sri Aurobindo
*The Synthesis of Yoga*

It seems to me that when you begin to see things in this way, when they appear to you as they are described here, you are already close, very close, to the solution.

The worst of it is that generally the whole material reality seems to be the only reality, and everything which is not that seems altogether secondary. And the "right" of that material consciousness to rule, guide, organise life, to dominate all the rest, is justified to such an extent that if someone tries to challenge this sacrosanct authority, he is considered half-mad or extremely dangerous.... It seems to me one must still go a very long way to consider material life in the way Sri Aurobindo has described it here. And I am quite convinced that if one feels it like that, sees it like that, as he has described it, one is very, very close to the remedy.

It is only *élite* natures, those who have already had a contact with a higher reality, with something of the divine Consciousness, who feel earthly existence in that way. And when one can become so fully conscious of all these weaknesses and stupidities of the outer consciousness, all these falsehoods of so-called material knowledge and so-called physical laws, the so-called necessities of the body, the "reality" of one's needs; if one begins to see how very false, stupid, illusory, obscure, foolish all this is, one is truly very close to the solution.

That is the impression I had while reading this.... I had the feeling that to see things in this way, one must have already climbed to a very high peak, and that one is at the gates of liberation....

If you can read this passage again and be convinced of its reality and its absolute truth, well, that is already a great step.[12]

THE MOTHER

## 8. Inner State and Outer Circumstances

... what we have within us creates the circumstances outside us.[13]

SRI AUROBINDO

Always circumstances come to reveal the hidden weaknesses that have to be overcome.[14]

THE MOTHER

When one does sadhana it is constantly seen that so long as there is an important defect somewhere, circumstances so happen that the occasion comes for the defect to rise until it is thrown out of the being. If one can take the coming of these circumstances clairvoyantly as a call and an opportunity for conquering the defect, then one can progress very quickly.[15]

SRI AUROBINDO

When the soul is meant to go forward and there is an external weakness..., circumstances do come... to help the external being against itself... there must be a truly sincere aspiration behind; otherwise it does not happen.[16]

SRI AUROBINDO

When someone is destined for the Path, all circumstances through all the deviations of mind and life help in one way or another to lead him to it. It is his own psychic being within him and Divine Power above that use to that end the vicissitudes both of mind and outward circumstance.[17]

SRI AUROBINDO

If you are in a state of conscious aspiration and very sincere, well, everything around you will be arranged in order to help in your aspiration, whether directly or indirectly, that is, either to make you progress, put you in touch with something new or to eliminate from your nature something that has to disappear. This is something quite remarkable. If you are truly in a state of intensity of aspiration, there is not a circumstance which does not come to help you to realise this aspiration. Everything comes, everything, as though there were a perfect and absolute consciousness organising around you all things, and you yourself in your outer ignorance may not recognise it and may protest at first against the circumstances as they show themselves, may complain, may try to change them; but after a while, when you have become wiser, and there is a certain distance between you and the event, well, you will realise that it was just what you needed to do to make the necessary progress. And, you know, it is a will, a supreme goodwill which arranges all things around you, and even when you complain and protest instead of accepting, it is exactly at such moments that it acts most effectively.

... If you say to the Divine with conviction, "I want only You", the Divine will arrange all the circumstances in such a way as to compel you to be sincere. Something in the being... "I want only You."... the aspiration... and then one wants a hundred odd things all the time, isn't that so? At times something comes, just... usually to disturb everything – it stands in the way and prevents you from realising your aspiration. Well, the Divine will come without showing Himself, without your seeing Him, without your having any inkling of it, and He will arrange all the circumstances in such a way that everything that prevents you from belonging solely to the Divine will be removed from your path, inevitably. Then when all is removed, you begin to howl and complain; but later, if you are sincere and look at yourself straight in the eye... you have said to the Lord, you have said, "I want only You." He will remain close to you, all the rest will go away. This is indeed a higher Grace. Only, you must say this with conviction. I don't even mean that you must say it integrally, because if one says it integrally, the work is done. What is necessary is that one part of the being, indeed the central will, says it with conviction: "I want only You." Even once, and it suffices: all that takes more or less long, sometimes it stretches over years, but one reaches the goal.

*But one has all kinds of imperfections!*

Eh? The more the imperfections, the longer it takes; the more the attachments one has, the longer it takes.
BUT THE GOAL IS SURE![18]

THE MOTHER

## 9. The Meaning of Circumstances

It is quite obvious that this world is full of suffering, and afflicted with transience to a degree that seems to justify the Gita's description of it as "this unhappy and transient world", *anityam asukham*. The question is whether it is a mere creation of Chance or governed by a mechanical inconscient Law or whether there is a meaning in it and something beyond its present appearance towards which we move. If there is a meaning and if there is something towards which things are evolving, then inevitably there must be a guidance – and that means that a supporting Consciousness and Will is there with which we can come into inner contact. If there is such a Consciousness and Will, it is not likely that it would stultify itself by annulling the world's meaning or turning it into a perpetual or eventual failure.

This world has a double aspect. It seems to be based on a material Inconscience and an ignorant mind and life full of that Inconscience: error and sorrow, death and suffering are the necessary consequence. But there is evidently too a partially successful endeavour and an imperfect growth towards Light, Knowledge, Truth, Good, Happiness, Harmony, Beauty, – at least a partial flowering of these things. The meaning of this world must evidently lie in this opposition; it must be an evolution which is leading or struggling towards higher things out of a first darker appearance. Whatever guidance there is must be given under these conditions of opposition and struggle and must be leading towards that higher state of things. It is leading the individual, certainly, and the world, presumably, towards the higher state, but through the double terms of knowledge and ignorance, light and darkness, death and life, pain and pleasure, happiness and suffering; none of the terms can be excluded until the higher status is reached and established. It is not and cannot be, ordinarily, a guidance which at once rejects the darker terms, still less a guidance which brings us solely and always nothing but happiness, success and good fortune. Its main concern is with the growth of our being and consciousness, the growth towards a higher self, towards the Divine, eventually towards a higher Light, Truth and Bliss; the rest is secondary, sometimes a means, sometimes a result, not a primary purpose.

The true sense of the guidance becomes clearer when we can go deep within and see from there more intimately the play of the forces and receive intimations of the Will behind them. The surface mind can get only an imperfect glimpse. When we are in contact with the Divine or in contact with an inner knowledge and vision, we begin to see all the circumstances of our life in a new light and can observe how they all tended, without our knowing it, towards the growth of our being and consciousness, towards the work we had to do, towards some development that had to be made, – not only what seemed good, fortunate or successful but also the struggles, failures, difficulties, upheavals. But with each person the guidance works differently according to his nature, the conditions of his life, his cast of consciousness, his stage of development, his need of further experience. We are not automata but conscious beings and our mentality, our will and its decisions, our attitude to life and demand on it, our motives and movements help to determine our course: they may lead to much suffering and evil, but through it all, the guidance makes use of them for our growth in experience and consequently the development of our being and consciousness. All advance, by however devious ways, even in spite of what seems a going backwards or going astray, gathering whatever experience is necessary for the soul's destiny. When we are in close contact with the Divine, a protection can come which helps or directly guides or moves us: it does not throw aside all difficulties, sufferings or dangers, but it carries us through them and out of them – except where for a special purpose there is need of the opposite.[19]

SRI AUROBINDO

When you are in a particular set of circumstances and certain events take place, these events often oppose your desire or what seems best to you, and often you happen to regret this and say to yourself, "Ah! how good it would have been if it were otherwise, if it had been like this or like that", for little things and big things.... Then years pass by, events are unfolded; you progress, become more conscious, understand better, and when you look back, you notice – first with astonishment, then later with a smile – that those very circumstances which seemed to you quite disastrous or unfavourable, were exactly the best thing that could have happened to you to make you progress as you should have. And if you are the least bit wise you tell yourself, "Truly, the divine Grace is infinite."

So, when this sort of thing has happened to you a number of times, you begin to understand that in spite of the blindness of man and deceptive appearances, the Grace is at work everywhere, so that at every moment it is the best possible thing that happens in the state the world is in at that moment. It is because our vision is limited or even because we are blinded by our own preferences that we cannot discern that things are like this.

But when one begins to see it, one enters upon a state of wonder which nothing can describe. For behind the appearances one perceives this Grace – infinite, wonderful, all-powerful – which knows all, organises all, arranges all, and leads us, whether we like it or not, whether we know it or not, towards the supreme goal, that is, union with the Divine, the awareness of the Godhead and union with Him.

Then one lives in the Action and Presence of the Grace a life full of joy, of wonder, with the feeling of a marvellous strength, and at the same time with a trust so calm, so complete, that nothing can shake it any longer.

And when one is in this state of perfect receptivity and perfect adherence, one diminishes to that extent the resistance of the world to the divine Action; consequently, this is the best collaboration one can bring to the Action of the Divine. One understands what He wants and, with all one's consciousness, adheres to His Will.[20]

THE MOTHER

*O Misfortune, blessed be thou; for through thee I have seen the face of my Lover.*

Sri Aurobindo
*Thoughts and Aphorisms*

*If through misfortune one sees the face of God, then it is no longer misfortune, is it?*

Obviously, far from being a misfortune, it is a blessing. And this is precisely what Sri Aurobindo means.

When things happen which are not what we expect, what we hope for, what we want, which are contrary to our desires, in our ignorance we call them misfortunes and lament. But if we were to become a little wiser and observe the deeper consequences of these very same events, we would find that they are leading us rapidly towards the Divine, the Beloved; whereas easy and pleasant circumstances encourage us to dally on the path, to stop along the way to pluck the flowers of pleasure which present themselves to us and which we are too weak or not sincere enough to reject resolutely, so that our march forward is not delayed.

One must already be very strong, very far along the way, to be able to face success and the little enjoyments it brings without giving way. Those who can do this, those who are strong, do not run after success; they do not seek it, and accept it with indifference. For they know and appreciate the value of the lashes given by unhappiness and misfortune.

But ultimately the true attitude, the sign and proof that we are near the goal, is a perfect equality which enables us to accept success and failure, fortune and misfortune, happiness and sorrow with the same tranquil joy; for all these things become marvellous gifts that the Lord in his infinite solicitude showers upon us.[21]

THE MOTHER

To be free from all preference and receive joyfully whatever comes from the Divine Will is not possible at first for any human being. What one should have at first is the constant idea that what the Divine wills is always for the best even when the mind does not see how it is so, to accept with resignation what one cannot yet accept with gladness and so to arrive at a calm equality which is not shaken even when on the surface there may be passing movements of a momentary reaction to outward happenings. If that is once firmly founded, the rest can come.[22]

SRI AUROBINDO

## 10.  Living Within

To live within, in constant aspiration towards the Divine – that renders us capable of regarding life with a smile and remaining in peace whatever the external circumstances.[23]

THE MOTHER

Live within, do not be shaken by external circumstances.[24]

THE MOTHER

He who lives to serve the Truth is not affected by outward circumstances.[25]

THE MOTHER

You have only to remain quiet and firm in your following of the path and your will to go to the end. If you do that circumstances will in the end be obliged to shape themselves to your will, because it will be the Divine Will in you.[26]

SRI AUROBINDO

Remain fixed in the sunlight of the true consciousness – for only there is happiness and peace. They do not depend upon outside happenings, but on this alone.[27]

SRI AUROBINDO

## 11. Meditations on Circumstances

Every morning my aspiration rises ardently to Thee, and in the silence of my satisfied heart I ask that Thy law of Love may be expressed, that Thy will may manifest. And in anticipation I adhere with joy and serenity to those circumstances which will express this law and this will.

Oh, why be restless and want that for oneself things should turn out in one way and not another! Why decide that a particular set of circumstances will be the expression of the best possibilities and then launch into a bitter struggle so that these possibilities may be realised! Why not use all one's energy solely to will in the calm of inner confidence that Thy law may triumph everywhere and always over all difficulties, all darkness, all egoism! How the horizon widens as soon as one learns to take this attitude; how all anxiety vanishes giving place to a constant illumination, to the omnipotence of disinterestedness! To will what Thou willest, O Lord, is to live constantly in communion with Thee, to be delivered from all contingencies, to escape all narrowness, to fill one's lungs with pure and wholesome air, to get rid of all useless weariness, be relieved of all cumbrous loads, so as to run briskly towards the only goal worth attaining: the triumph of Thy divine Law!

O Lord, with what joy and trust I greet Thee this morning!...[28]

THE MOTHER

This morning, as I was glancing over the month that is beginning and wondering how I could serve Thee better, I heard the small voice within like a murmur in the silence, and this is what it said to me: "See how very little all outer circumstances matter. Why strive and strain so to realise thy own conception of Truth? Be more supple, more trusting. The only duty is not to let oneself be troubled by anything. To torment oneself about doing the right thing causes as much harm as a bad will. Only in a calm as of deep waters can be found the possibility of True Service."

And this reply was so luminous and pure, it carried within itself such a striking reality, that the state it described was communicated without any difficulty. It seemed to me I was floating in the calm of deep waters; I understood; I saw clearly what the best attitude would be; and now I have only to ask Thee, O Sublime Master, my Supreme Teacher, to give me the strength and clear-sightedness I need to remain constantly in this state.

"Do not torment thyself, child. Silence, peace, peace."[29]

THE MOTHER

O Lord, my one aspiration is to know Thee and serve Thee better every day. What do outer circumstances matter? They seem to me each day more vain and illusory, and I take less and less interest in what is going to happen to us in the outer life; but more and more am I intensely interested in the one thing which seems important to me: To know Thee better in order to serve Thee better. All outer events must converge upon this goal and this goal alone; and for that all depends upon the attitude we have towards them. To seek Thee constantly in all things, to want to manifest Thee ever better in every circumstance, in this attitude lies supreme Peace, perfect serenity, true contentment. In it life blossoms, widens, expands so magnificently in such majestic waves that no storm can any longer disturb it.

O Lord, Thou art our safeguard, our only happiness, Thou art our resplendent light, our pure love, our hope and our strength. Thou art our life, the reality of our being!

In a reverent and joyful adoration I bow to Thee.[30]

THE MOTHER

Thou art perfect knowledge, absolute consciousness. He who unites with Thee is omniscient – while the union lasts. But even before attaining this stage, he who has given himself to Thee in all the sincerity of his being, with all his conscious will, he who has resolved to make every effort to help in the manifestation and triumph of Thy divine law of Love in himself and the whole field of his influence, sees all things in his life change, and all circumstances begin to express Thy law and assist his consecration: for him it is the best, the very best that always happens; and if in his intelligence there is still some obscurity, some ignorant desire which at times prevents him from becoming aware of it immediately, he recognises sooner or later that a beneficent power seemed to protect him even from himself and secure for him conditions most favourable to his blossoming and transfiguration, his integral conversion and utilisation.

As soon as one becomes conscious and convinced of this, one can no longer worry about future circumstances or the turn events take; it is with perfect serenity that one does at every moment what one thinks best, convinced that the best too is sure to come from it, even if it is not the result which we, with our limited reasoning, expected from it.

That is why, Lord, our heart is light, our thought in repose. That is why we turn to Thee in all confidence and say peacefully:

May Thy will be done, in it true harmony is realised.[31]

THE MOTHER

# II

# LOOKING AT ONESELF AND OTHERS

# LOOKING AT ONESELF AND OTHERS

## 1. Discovering a Hidden Treasure

*We should seek the company of the sage who shows our faults, as if he were showing us a hidden treasure.*

The Dhammapada

In all Scriptures meant to help mankind to progress, it is always said that you must be very grateful to those who show you your faults and so you must seek their company; but the form used here is particularly felicitous: if a fault is shown to you it is as if a treasure were shown to you; that is to say, each time that you discover in yourself a fault, incapacity, lack of understanding, weakness, insincerity, all that prevents you from making a progress, it is as if you discovered a wonderful treasure.

Instead of growing sad and telling yourself, "Oh, there is still another defect", you should, on the contrary, rejoice as if you had made a wonderful acquisition, because you have just caught hold of one of those things that prevented you from progressing. And once you have caught hold of it, pull it out! For those who practise a yogic discipline consider that the moment you know that a thing should not be, you have the power to remove it, discard it, destroy it.

To discover a fault is an acquisition. It is as though a flood of light had come to replace the little speck of obscurity which has just been driven out.[32]

THE MOTHER

But that [not recognising one's defects] is a very common human weakness, although it ought not to exist in a sadhak whose progress depends largely on his recognising what has to be changed in him. Not that the recognition by itself is sufficient, but it is a necessary element. It is of course a kind of pride or vanity which considers this necessary for strength and standing. Not only will they not recognise it before others but they hide their defects from themselves or even if obliged to look at it with one eye look away from it with the other. Or they weave a veil of words and excuses and justifications trying to make it something other than it really is.[33]

SRI AUROBINDO

That is a great error of the human vital – to want compliments for their own sake and to be depressed by their absence and imagine that it means there is no capacity. In this world one starts with ignorance and imperfection in whatever one does – one has to find out one's mistakes and to learn, one has to commit errors and find out by correcting them the right way to do things. Nobody in the world has ever escaped from this law. So what one has to expect from others is not compliments all the time, but praise of what is right or well done and criticism of errors and mistakes. The more one can bear criticism and see one's mistakes, the more likely one is to arrive at the fullness of one's capacity.

As for comparison with others, one ought not to do that. Each one has his own lesson to learn, his own work to do and he must concern himself with that, not with the superior or inferior progress of others in comparison with himself. If he is behind today, he can be in full capacity hereafter and it is for that future perfection of his powers that he must labour....

But learn to welcome criticism and the pointing out of imperfections – the more you do so, the more rapidly you will advance.[34]

SRI AUROBINDO

To recognise one's weaknesses and false movements and draw back from them is the way towards liberation.[35]

SRI AUROBINDO

## 2. Turning to the Coming Light

It is necessary to observe and know the wrong movements in you; for they are the source of your trouble and have to be persistently rejected if you are to be free.

But do not be always thinking of your defects and wrong movements. Concentrate more upon what you are to be, on the ideal, with the faith that, since it is the goal before you, it must and will come.

To be always observing faults and wrong movements brings depression and discourages the faith. Turn your eyes more to the coming light and less to any immediate darkness. Faith, cheerfulness, confidence in the ultimate victory are the things that help, – they make the progress easier and swifter.[36]

SRI AUROBINDO

... one must not be distressed or depressed by perceiving the weaknesses inherent in human nature and the difficulty of getting them out. The difficulty is natural, for they have been there for thousands of lives and are the very nature of man's vital and mental ignorance. It is not surprising that they should have a power to stick and take time to disappear. But there is a true being and a true consciousness that is there in us hidden by the surface formations of nature and which can shake them off once it emerges. By taking the right attitude of selfless devotion within and persisting in it in spite of the surface nature's troublesome self-repetitions one enables this inner being and consciousness to emerge and with the Mother's Force, working in it deliver the being from all return of the movements of the old nature.[37]

SRI AUROBINDO

Humility is needful, but constant self-depreciation does not help; excessive self-esteem and self-depreciation are both wrong attitudes. To recognise any defects without exaggerating them is useful but, once recognised, it is no good dwelling on them always; you must have the confidence that the Divine Force can change everything and you must let the Force work.[38]

SRI AUROBINDO

*Is blaming oneself a good method of progressing?*

... No, not necessarily. It may be useful, it is indeed useful from time to time in order to get out of the illusion of one's own perfection. But one wastes much energy in self-criticism. It is much better to use this same energy in making progress, a concrete progress, something more useful. For example, if you have thoughts which are unpleasant, ugly, vulgar and disturbing, and you say, "Ah, ah, how intolerable I am, I still have such thoughts, what a nuisance it is!", it would be much better to use this very energy simply to do this (*gesture*) and drive away the thoughts.

And this is only the first step. The second is to try to have other thoughts, to take interest in something else: either read or reflect, but in any case try to fill your mind with something more interesting, to use your energy in constructing rather than in destroying.

It is of course necessary from time to time to recognise one's faults; it is altogether indispensable. But to dwell too much upon them is not necessary. What is necessary is to use all one's energy in order to build up the qualities one wants to have and do what one wants to do. This is much more important.[39]

THE MOTHER

### 3. Defects of Others

Do not dwell much on the defects of others. It is not helpful. Keep always quiet and peace in the attitude.[40]

SRI AUROBINDO

Only those who sympathise can help – surely also one

should be able to see the faults of others without hatred. Hatred injures both parties, it helps none.[41]

SRI AUROBINDO

There is no harm in seeing and observing if it is done with sympathy and impartiality – it is the tendency unnecessarily to criticise, find fault, condemn others (often quite wrongly) which creates a bad atmosphere both for oneself and others. And why this harshness and cocksure condemnation? Has not each man his own faults – why should he be so eager to find fault with others and condemn them? Sometimes one has to judge but it should not be done hastily or in a censorious spirit.[42]

SRI AUROBINDO

Men are always more able to criticise sharply the work of others and tell them how to do things or what not to do than skilful to avoid the same mistakes themselves. Often indeed one sees easily in others faults which are there in oneself but which one fails to see.... The human mind is not really conscious of itself – that is why in yoga one has always to look and see what is in oneself and become more and more conscious.[43]

SRI AUROBINDO

Not to judge anyone but oneself until one can see things from a calm mind and a calm vital is an excellent rule. Also, do not allow your mind to form hasty impressions

on the strength of some outward appearance, nor your
vital to act upon them.

There is a place in the inner being where one can always
remain calm and from there look with poise and judgment
on the perturbations of the surface consciousness and act
upon it to change it. If you can learn to live in that calm of
the inner being, you will have found your stable basis.[44]

SRI AUROBINDO

## 4. Equality, Goodwill

There are two attitudes that a sadhak can have: either a
quiet equality to all regardless of their friendliness or
hostility or a general goodwill.[45]

SRI AUROBINDO

... what you should do is to keep your right attitude
towards the others and not allow yourself to be upset,
irritated or displeased by anything they may say or do – in
other words keep the *samatā* and universal goodwill
proper to a sadhak of yoga. If you do that and still others
get upset or displeased, you must not mind as you will not
be responsible for their wrong reaction.[46]

SRI AUROBINDO

This [misunderstanding between two minds] can only be
cured by a change of consciousness – for when one goes
into a deeper consciousness, first, one sees the cause of

these things and is not troubled, – one acquires an understanding, patience and tolerance that makes one free from
vexation and other reactions. If both or all grow in
consciousness, then there arises a mental understanding of
each other's viewpoints which makes it easier to bring in
harmony and smooth working. It is this that should be
sought by the change within – to create the same harmony
from outside by exterior means is not so easy, as the
human mind is stiff in its perceptions and the human vital
insistent on its own way of action. Let this be your main
will – to grow yourself within and let the clearer and
deeper consciousness come and have a goodwill for the
same change to come in others so that charity and
harmony may come in the place of friction and misunder-
standing.[47]

Sri Aurobindo

Always be kind and you will be free from suffering, always
be contented and happy, and you will radiate your quiet
happiness.

It is particularly noticeable that all the digestive functions are extremely sensitive to an attitude that is critical,
bitter, full of ill-will, to a sour judgment. Nothing disturbs
the functioning of the digestion more than that. And it is a
vicious circle: the more the digestive function is disturbed,
the more unkind you become, critical, dissatisfied with life
and things and people. So you can't find any way out. And
there is only one cure: to deliberately drop this attitude, to
absolutely forbid yourself to have it and to impose upon
yourself, by constant self-control, a deliberate attitude of

all-comprehending kindness. Just try and you will see that you feel much better.[48]

THE MOTHER

A contempt for others is out of place, especially since the Divine is in all. Evidently, the activities and aspirations of men are not trivial and worthless, for all life is a growth of the soul out of the darkness towards the Light. But our attitude is that humanity cannot grow out of its limitations by the ordinary means adopted by the human mind, politics, social reform, philanthropy, etc. – these can only be temporary or local palliatives. The only true escape is a change of consciousness, a change into a greater, wider and purer way of being, and a life and action based upon that change. It is therefore to that that the energies must be turned, once the spiritual orientation is complete. This implies no contempt, but the preference of the only effective means over those which have been found in-effective.[49]

SRI AUROBINDO

No doubt, hatred and cursing are not the proper attitude. It is true also that to look upon all things and all people with a calm and clear vision, to be uninvolved and impartial in one's judgments is a quite proper yogic attitude. A condition of perfect *samatā* can be established in which one sees all as equal, friends and enemies included, and is not disturbed by what men do or by what happens. The question is whether this is all that is

demanded from us. If so, then the general attitude will be
of a neutral indifference to everything. But the Gita,
which strongly insists on a perfect and absolute *samatā*,
goes on to say, "Fight, destroy the adversary, conquer." If
there is no kind of general action wanted, no loyalty to
Truth as against Falsehood except for one's personal
sadhana, no will for the Truth to conquer, then the *samatā*
of indifference will suffice. But here there is a work to be
done, a Truth to be established against which immense
forces are arranged, invisible forces which can use visible
things and persons and actions for their instruments. If
one is among the disciples, the seekers of this Truth, one
has to take sides for the Truth, to stand against the forces
that attack it and seek to stifle it. Arjuna wanted not to
stand for either side, to refuse any action of hostility even
against assailants; Sri Krishna, who insisted so much on
*samatā*, strongly rebuked his attitude and insisted equally
on his fighting the adversary. "Have *samatā*," he said,
"and seeing clearly the Truth, fight." Therefore to take
sides with the Truth and to refuse to concede anything to
the Falsehood that attacks, to be unflinchingly loyal and
against the hostiles and the attackers, is not inconsistent
with equality. It is personal and egoistic feeling that has to
be thrown away; hatred and vital ill-will have to be
rejected. But loyalty and refusal to compromise with the
assailants and the hostiles or to dally with their ideas and
demands and say, "After all, we can compromise with
what they ask from us", or to accept them as companions
and our own people – these things have a great importance.... It is a spiritual battle inward and outward; by
neutrality and compromise or even passivity one may
allow the enemy forces to pass and crush down the Truth

and its children. If you look at it from this point, you will
see that if the inner spiritual equality is right, the active
loyalty and firm taking of sides is as right, and the two
cannot be incompatible.[50]

SRI AUROBINDO

## 5. Dealing with Others

To take advantage of what is good in others, keeping
one's eye always on that, and to deal tactfully with their
mistakes, faults and defects is the best way; it does not
exclude firmness and maintenance of discipline, even
severity when severity is due; but the latter should be rare
and the others should not feel it as if it were a permanent
attitude.[51]

SRI AUROBINDO

... each human being is composed of different persona-
lities that feel and behave in a different way and his action
is determined by the one that happens to be prominent at
the time. The one that has no feelings against anyone is
either the psychic being or the emotional being in the
heart, the one that feels anger and is severe is a part of the
external vital nature on the surface. This anger and
severity is a wrong form of something that in itself has a
value, a certain strength of will and force of action and
control in the vital being, without which work cannot be
done. What is necessary is to get rid of the anger and to
keep the force and firm will along with a developed
judgment as to what is the right thing to do in any circum-

stances. For instance, people can be allowed to do things
in their own way when that does not spoil the work, when
it is only their way of doing what is necessary to be done;
when their way is opposed to the discipline of the work,
then they have to be controlled, but it should be done
quietly and kindly, not with anger.[52]

Sri Aurobindo

To discourage anybody is wrong, but to give false encouragement or encouragement of anything wrong is not
right. Severity has sometimes to be used (though not
overused), when without it an obstinate persistence in
what is wrong cannot be set right.[53]

Sri Aurobindo

It [disciplining the subordinates] has to be done in the
right spirit and the subordinates must be able to feel that it
is so – that they are being dealt with in all uprightness and
by a man who has sympathy and insight and not only
severity and energy. It is a question of vital tact and a
strong and large vital finding always the right way to deal
with the others.[54]

Sri Aurobindo

In dealing with others there is a way of speaking and doing
which gives most offence and opens one most to mis-
understanding and there is also a way which is quiet and
firm but conciliatory to those who can be conciliated – all
who are not absolutely of bad will. It is better to use the

latter than the former. No weakness, no arrogance or violence, this should be the spirit.[55]

SRI AUROBINDO

## 6. Sin – A Thing Not in its Right Place

*To hate the sinner is the worst sin, for it is hating God; yet he who commits it glories in his superior virtue.*

Sri Aurobindo
*Thoughts and Aphorisms*

*When we enter into a certain state of consciousness, we see clearly that we are capable of anything and that in fact there is not a single "sin" that is not potentially our sin. Is this impression correct? And yet we revolt against and feel an aversion for certain things: there is always something somewhere which we cannot accept. Why? What is the true attitude, the effective attitude in face of evil?*

There is not a single sin that is not our sin.... You have this experience when for some reason or other – depending on the case – you come into contact with the universal state of consciousness – not in its limitless essence, but on any level of Matter. There is an atomic consciousness; there is a purely material consciousness; and there is, even more, a general psychological consciousness. When by going within, by a kind of withdrawal from the ego, you come into contact with this zone of consciousness, let us say, a terrestrial or collective human psychological zone –

there is a difference, "collective human" is restrictive, whereas "terrestrial" includes many animal movements, even plant movements; but as in the present case the moral notion of guilt, sin, evil belongs exclusively to the human consciousness, we will say simply the collective human psychological consciousness – when you come into contact with that through this identification, naturally you feel or see or know that you are capable of any human movement anywhere. It is to some extent a truth-consciousness – this egoistic sense of what belongs and does not belong to you, of what you can do and cannot do, disappears at that time; you become aware that the fundamental structure of the human consciousness is such that any human being is capable of doing anything at all. And since you are in a truth-consciousness, at the same time you have the feeling that judgments or aversions, or rejection, are absurd. *Everything* is potentially there. And if certain currents of force – which you usually cannot trace; you see them come and go, but as a rule their origin and direction are unknown – if any one of these currents enters into you, it can make you do anything.

If you could always remain in this state of consciousness, after some time – provided you maintained within you the flame of Agni, the flame of purification and progress – you would be able not only to prevent these movements from taking an active form in you and expressing themselves materially, but also to act on the very nature of the movement and transform it. But, of course, unless you have attained a very high degree of realisation, it will be practically impossible to maintain this state of consciousness for long. Almost immediately you fall back into the egoistic consciousness of the separate self. And then all the difficulties come back: the disgust, the revolt against certain things, the horror they arouse in you, etc.

It is probable – it is even certain – that until you are yourself completely transformed, these movements of disgust and revolt are needed so that you can do *in yourself* what has to be done to shut the door. For after all, the problem is not to allow them to manifest themselves.

In another aphorism Sri Aurobindo says – I no longer remember his exact words – that sin is merely something which is not in its right place. In this perpetual Becoming nothing ever repeats itself, and there are things that disappear, so to speak, into the past; and when their disappearance becomes necessary these things become, for our very limited consciousness, bad and repulsive. And we revolt against them because their time is over. But if we had the overall view, if we could contain within ourselves the past, the present and the future all at once – as it is somewhere above – we would see the relativity of these things and that it is above all the progressive Force of evolution that gives us the will to reject; and that wherever they are in their right place, they are quite acceptable. Only, it is practically impossible to have this experience unless you have the total vision, that is to say, the vision that belongs to the Supreme alone! Therefore you must first of all identify yourself with the Supreme; then, afterwards, with this identification, you can return to a sufficiently exteriorised consciousness and see things as they are. But that is the principle, and to the extent that you are capable of realising it, you reach a state of consciousness where you can look at everything with a smile of total certitude that everything is as it should be....

Basically, disgust, revolt, anger, all these movements of violence are necessarily movements of ignorance and limitation, with all the weakness that limitation represents. Revolt is a weakness – it is the feeling of an impotent will. You will – or you think you will – you feel, you see that things are not as they should be and you revolt against whatever does not agree with what you see. But if you were all-powerful, if your will and your vision were all-powerful, there would be no occasion for you to revolt, you would always see that all things are as they should be. If we go to the highest level and unite with the consciousness of the supreme Will, we see, at every second, at every moment of the universe, that all is exactly as it should be, exactly as the Supreme wills it. That is omnipotence. And all movements of violence become not only unnecessary but utterly ridiculous.

Therefore there is only one solution: to unite ourselves by aspiration, concentration, interiorisation and identification with the supreme Will. And that is both omnipotence and perfect freedom at the same time. And that is the only omnipotence and the only freedom; everything else is an approximation. You may be on the way, but it is not the entire thing. So if you experience this, you realise that with this supreme freedom and supreme power there is also a total peace and a serenity that never fails. Therefore, if you feel something which is not that, a revolt, a disgust, something which you cannot accept, it means that *in you* there is a part which has not been touched by the transformation, something which has kept the old consciousness, something which is still on the path – that is all.[56]

THE MOTHER

## 7. Helping Others

... each one – this totality of substance constituting your inner and outer body, the totality of substance with which your being is built from the outermost to the inmost – is a field of work; it is as though one had gathered together carefully, accumulated a certain number of vibrations and put them at your disposal for you to work upon them fully. It is like a field of action constantly at your disposal: night and day, waking or asleep, all the time – nobody can take it away from you, it is wonderful! You may refuse to use it (as most men do), but it is a mass to be transformed that is there in your hands, fully at your disposal, given to you for you to learn to work upon it. So, the most important thing is to begin by doing that. You can do nothing with others unless you are able to do it with yourself. You can never give a good advice to anyone unless you are able to give it to yourself first, and to follow it. And if you see a difficulty somewhere, the best way of changing this difficulty is to change it in yourself first. If you see a defect in anyone, you may be sure it is in you, and you begin to change it in yourself. And when you will have changed it in yourself, you will be strong enough to change it in others. And this is a wonderul thing, people don't realise what an infinite grace it is that this universe is arranged in such a way that there is a collection of substance, from the most material to the highest spiritual, all that gathered together into what is called a small individual, but at the disposal of a central Will. And that is yours, your field of work, nobody can take it away from you, it is your own property. And to the extent you can work upon it, you will be able to have an action upon the world. But only to that extent. One must do more for oneself, besides, than one does for others.[57]

THE MOTHER

If one sincerely wants to help others and the world, the best thing one can do is to be oneself what one wants others to be – not only as an example, but because one becomes a centre of radiating power which, by the very fact that it exists, compels the rest of the world to transform itself.[58]

THE MOTHER

To concentrate most on one's own spiritual growth and experience is the first necessity of the sadhak – to be eager to help others draws away from the inner work. To grow in the spirit is the greatest help one can give to others, for then something flows out naturally to those around that helps them.[59]

SRI AUROBINDO

# III

# ACTION AND WORK

# ACTION AND WORK

## 1. Acting from Within

Not only in your inward concentration, but in your outward acts and movements you must take the right attitude.[60]

SRI AUROBINDO

You must learn to act always from within – from your inner being…. The outer should be a mere instrument and should not be allowed at all to compel or dictate your speech, thought or action.[61]

SRI AUROBINDO

All should be done quietly from within – working, speaking, reading, writing as part of the real consciousness – not with the dispersed and unquiet movement of the ordinary consciousness.[62]

SRI AUROBINDO

It is the spirit and the consciousness from which it is done that makes an action yogic – it is not the action itself.[63]

SRI AUROBINDO

Everything depends on the inner condition, and the outward action is only useful as a means and a help for expressing or confirming the inner condition and making it dynamic and effective. If you do or say a thing with the psychic uppermost or with the right inner touch, it will be effective; if you do or say the same thing out of the mind or the vital or with a wrong or mixed atmosphere, it may be quite ineffective. To do the right thing in the right way in each case and at each moment one must be in the right consciousness – it can't be done by following a fixed mental rule....[64]

SRI AUROBINDO

## 2. Choice of Work

*What is my place in the universal work?*

We all have a role to fulfil, a work to accomplish, a place which we alone can occupy.

But since this work is the expression, the outer manifestation of the inmost depth of our being, we can become conscious of its definitive form only when we become conscious of this depth within ourselves.

This is what sometimes happens in cases of true conversion.

The moment we perceive the transfiguring light and give ourselves to it without reserve, we can suddenly and precisely become aware of what we are made for, of the purpose of our existence on earth.

But this enlightenment is exceptional. It is brought about within us by a whole series of efforts and inner attitudes. And one of the essential conditions if we want to achieve and maintain within ourselves these attitudes, these soul-states, is to devote part of our time each day to some impersonal action; every day, we must do something useful for others.

Until we know *the* essential thing we are intended to do, we must therefore find a temporary occupation which will be the best possible manifestation of our present capacities and our goodwill.

Then we shall give ourselves to this occupation with conscientiousness and perseverance, knowing that it may well be only a stage and that with the progress of our ideal and our energies, we shall certainly one day be led to see more clearly the work we must accomplish. To the extent that we lose the habit of referring everything to ourselves and learn more and more to give ourselves more completely, with greater love, to earth and men, we shall see our horizons widen and our duties become more numerous and clear.

We shall find that our action follows a general line of progression determined by our own particular temperament.

Indeed, the successive occupations we shall hold before we become conscious of the definitive form of our action will always point in the same direction, be of the same type and mode, which is the spontaneous expression of our character, our nature, our own characteristic vibration.

The discovery of this tendency, this particular orientation, should come about quite naturally; it is a matter of taste and free choice, beyond all outer selfish considerations.

People are often blamed for choosing an action for themselves which does not correspond to their abilities. There is a slight confusion here.

Those who freely set out to accomplish their own favourite work cannot, in my opinion, be on the wrong track; this work must surely be the expression of their own particular tendency. But their mistake lies in wanting to accomplish this work all at once in its entirety, in its integrality, in depth and above all on the surface, forgetting that the very conception of the work is imperfect as they are imperfect and that to be wise, they should add to the knowledge of what they *wish* to do the more immediate and practical knowledge of what they are *capable* of doing at the present moment.

By taking both these factors into account, they can employ themselves with a minimum waste of time and energy.

But few people act with so much insight and wisdom. And it very often happens that one who is seeking his way falls into one of these two possible errors:

Either he takes his desires for realities, that is, he over-estimates his present strength and capacity and imagines that he is capable of immediately assuming a place and a role which he can honourably fulfil only after many years of methodical and persevering effort.

Or he underestimates his latent powers and deliberately confines himself, in spite of his deeper aspirations, to a task which is far beneath his abilities and which will gradually extinguish within him the light that could have shone for others.

It seems difficult at first to steer clear of these pitfalls and find the balanced way, the middle way.

But we have a sure pointer to guide us.

Above all, whatever we undertake should not be done for the purpose of self-assertion. If we are attached to fame and glory, to the esteem of our peers, we are soon led to make concessions to them; and if we seek any opportunity to admire ourselves, it becomes easy to make ourselves out to be what we are not, and nothing more obscures the ideal within us.

We should never tell ourselves, openly or indirectly, "I want to be great, what vocation can I find for myself in order to become great?"

On the contrary, we should tell ourselves, "There must certainly be something I can do better than anyone else, since each one of us is a special mode of manifestation of the divine power which, in its essence, is one in all. However humble and modest it may be, this is precisely the thing to which I should devote myself, and in order to find it, I shall observe and analyse my tastes, tendencies and preferences, and I shall do it without pride or excessive humility, whatever others may think I shall do it just as I breathe, just as the flower smells sweet, quite simply, quite naturally, because I cannot do otherwise."

As soon as we have abolished within us, even for a moment, all egoistic desires, all personal and selfish aims, we can surrender to this inner spontaneity, this deep inspiration which will enable us to commune with the living and progressive forces of the universe.

The conception of our work will inevitably grow more perfect as we grow more perfect ourselves; and to realise this growing perfection, no effort to exceed ourselves should be neglected, but the work we perform must become always more and more joyful and spontaneous, like water welling from a pure spring.[65]

THE MOTHER

There is no need for you to change the line of life and work you have chosen so long as you feel that to be the way of your nature (*svabhāva*) or dictated to you by your inner being or, for some reason, it is seen to be your proper dharma. These are the three tests and apart from that I do not know if there is any fixed line of conduct or way of work or life that can be laid down for the yoga of the Gita. It is the spirit or consciousness in which the work is done that matters most; the outer form can vary greatly for different natures....[66]

SRI AUROBINDO

Work can be of two kinds – the work that is a field of experience used for the sadhana, for a progressive harmonisation and transformation of the being and its activities, and work that is a realised expression of the Divine. But the time for the latter can be only when the Realisation has been fully brought down into the earth-consciousness; till then all work must be a field of endeavour and a school of experience.[67]

SRI AUROBINDO

We must find the Self, the Divine, then only can we know what is the work the Self or the Divine demands from us. Until then our life and action can only be a help or means towards finding the Divine and it ought not to have any other purpose. As we grow in the inner consciousness, or as the spiritual Truth of the Divine grows in us, our life and action must indeed more and more flow from that, be one with that. But to decide beforehand by our limited

mental conceptions what they must be is to hamper the
growth of the spiritual Truth within.[68]

SRI AUROBINDO

Self-dedication does not depend on the particular work
you do, but on the spirit in which all work, of whatever
kind it may be, is done. Any work done well and carefully
as a sacrifice to the Divine, without desire or egoism, with
equality of mind and calm tranquillity in good or bad
fortune, for the sake of the Divine and not for the sake of
any personal gain, reward or result, with the consciousness that it is the Divine Power to which all work belongs,
is a means of self-dedication through Karma.[69]

SRI AUROBINDO

Of course the idea of bigness and smallness is quite
foreign to the spiritual truth.... Spiritually there is nothing
big or small. Such ideas are like those of the literary
people who think writing a poem is a high work and
making shoes or cooking the dinner is a small and low
one. But all is equal in the eyes of the Spirit – and it is
only the spirit within with which it is done that matters. It
is the same with a particular kind of work, there is nothing
big or small.[70]

SRI AUROBINDO

... one must take it [work done in the world] as a training
and do it in the spirit of Karmayoga – what matters there
is not the nature of the work in itself, but the spirit in

which it is done. It must be in the spirit of the Gita, without desire, with detachment, without repulsion, but doing it as perfectly as possible, not for the sake of the family or promotion or to please the superiors, but simply because it is the thing that has been given in the hand to do. It is a field of inner training, nothing else. One has to learn in it these things, equality, desirelessness, dedication. It is not the work as a thing for its own sake, but one's doing of it and one's way of doing it that one has to dedicate to the Divine. Done in that spirit, it does not matter what the work is.[71]

SRI AUROBINDO

It depends on a certain extension and intensifying of the consciousness by which all activity becomes interesting not for itself but because of the consciousness put into it and, through the intensity of the energy, there is a pleasure in the exercise of the energy, and in the perfect doing of the work, whatever the work may be.[72]

SRI AUROBINDO

## 3. The Work that Purifies

The spiritual effectivity of work... depends on the inner attitude.[73]

SRI AUROBINDO

The only work that spiritually purifies is that which is done without personal motives, without desire for fame or public recognition or worldly greatness, without insistence on one's own mental motives or vital lusts and demands or physical preferences, without vanity or crude self-assertion or claim for position or prestige.... All work done in an egoistic spirit, however good for people in the world of the Ignorance, is of no avail to the seeker of the yoga.[74]

Sri Aurobindo

Men usually work and carry on their affairs from the ordinary motives of the vital being, need, desire of wealth or success or position or power or fame or the push to activity and the pleasure of manifesting their capacities, and they succeed or fail according to their capability, power of work and the good or bad fortune which is the result of their nature and their Karma. When one takes up the yoga and wishes to consecrate one's life to the Divine, these ordinary motives of the vital being have no longer their full and free play; they have to be replaced by another, a mainly psychic and spiritual motive, which will enable the sadhak to work with the same force as before, no longer for himself, but for the Divine. If the ordinary vital motives or vital force can no longer act freely and yet are not replaced by something else, then the push or force put into the work may decline or the power to command success may no longer be there. For the sincere sadhak the difficulty can only be temporary; but he has to see the defect in his consciousness or his attitude and to remove it. Then the Divine Power itself will act through him and use his capacity and vital force for its ends.[75]

Sri Aurobindo

To be free from all egoistic motive, careful of truth in speech and action, void of self-will and self-assertion, watchful in all things, is the condition for being a flawless servant.[76]

Sri Aurobindo

... get the spirit of the yoga of works as it is indicated in the Gita – forget yourself and your miseries in the aspiration to a larger consciousness, feel the greater Force working in the world and make yourself an instrument for a work to be done, however small it may be. But, whatever the way may be, you must accept it wholly and put your whole will into it – with a divided and wavering will you cannot hope for success in anything, neither in life nor in yoga.[77]

Sri Aurobindo

## 4. Fatigue and Rest

When you feel tired, don't overstrain yourself but rest – doing only your ordinary work; restlessly doing something or other all the time is not the way to cure it. To be quiet without and within is what is needed when there is this sense of fatigue. There is always a strength near you which you can call in and will remove these things, but you must learn to be quiet in order to receive it.[78]

Sri Aurobindo

... it is a mistake to overstrain as there is a reaction

afterwards. If there is energy, all must not be spent, some must be stored up so as to increase the permanent strength of the system.[79]

SRI AUROBINDO

Think of your work only when it is being done, not before and not after.

Do not let your mind go back on a work that is finished. It belongs to the past and all re-handling of it is a waste of power.

Do not let your mind labour in anticipation on a work that has to be done. The Power that acts in you will see to it at its own time.

... If you can remember to let your mind work only when its action is needed, the strain will lessen and disappear.[80]

SRI AUROBINDO

... what does that [relaxation] mean for most men? It means, always, coming down to a lower level. They do not know that for a true relaxation one must rise one degree higher, one must rise above oneself. If one goes down, it adds to one's fatigue and brings a stupefaction. Besides, each time one comes down, one increases the load of the subconscient – this huge subconscient load which one must clean and clean if one wants to mount, and which is like fetters on the feet....

It is not by sinking below oneself that one removes fatigue. One must climb the ladder and there one has true rest, because one has the inner peace, the light, the universal energy. And little by little one puts oneself in touch with the truth which is the very reason of one's existence.

If you contact that definitively, it removes completely all fatigue.[81]

THE MOTHER

### 5. Handling Physical Things

There is a consciousness in each physical thing with which one can communicate. Everything has an individuality of a certain kind, houses, cars, furniture etc. The ancient peoples knew that and so they saw a spirit or "genius" in every physical thing.[82]

SRI AUROBINDO

What you feel about physical things is true – there is a consciousness in them, a life which is not the life and consciousness of man and animal which we know, but still secret and real. That is why we must have a respect for physical things and use them rightly, not misuse and waste, ill-treat or handle with a careless roughness. This feeling of all being consciousness or alive comes when our own physical consciousness – and not the mind only – awakes out of its obscurity and becomes aware of the One in all things, the Divine everywhere.[83]

SRI AUROBINDO

It is very true that physical things have a consciousness

within them which feels and responds to care and is sensitive to careless touch and rough handling. To know or feel that and learn to be careful of them is a great progress of consciousness.[84]

SRI AUROBINDO

The rough handling and careless breaking or waste and misuse of physical things is a denial of the yogic consciousness and a great hindrance to the bringing down of the Divine Truth to the material plane.[85]

SRI AUROBINDO

# IV

# ORDEALS AND DIFFICULTIES

# ORDEALS AND DIFFICULTIES

## 1. Difficulties Across the Path

There cannot be any high endeavour, least of all in the spiritual field, which does not raise or encounter grave obstacles of a very persistent character. These are both internal and external, and, although in the large they are fundamentally the same for all, there may be a great difference in the distribution of their stress or the outward form they take.[86]

SRI AUROBINDO

Yoga has always its difficulties, whatever yoga it be. Moreover, it acts in a different way on different seekers. Some have to overcome the difficulties of their nature first before they get any experiences to speak of, others get a splendid beginning and all the difficulties afterwards, others go on for a long time having alternate risings to the top of the wave and then a descent into the gulfs and so on till the difficulty is worked out, others have a smooth path which does not mean that they have no difficulties – they have plenty, but they do not care a straw for them, because they feel that the Divine will help them to the goal or that he is with them even when they do not feel him – their faith makes them imperturbable.[87]

SRI AUROBINDO

... there is always something that either carries us on or forces us on. This may take the shape of something conscious in front, the shape of a mastering spiritual idea, indestructible aspiration or fixed faith which may seem sometimes entirely veiled or even destroyed in periods of darkness or violent upheaval, but always they reappear when the storm has passed or the blackness of night has thinned, and reassert their influence. But also it may be something in the very essence of the being deeper than any idea or will in the mind, deeper and more permanent than the heart's aspiration but hidden from one's own observation. One who is moved to yoga by some curiosity of the mind or even by its desire for knowledge can turn aside from the path from disappointment or any other cause; still more can those who take it up from some inner ambition or vital desire turn away through revolt or frustration or the despondency of frequent check and failure. But if this deeper thing is there, then one cannot permanently leave the path of spiritual endeavour: one may decide to leave the path but is not allowed from within to do it or one may leave but is obliged to return to it by the secret spiritual need within him.

All these things are common to every path of yoga; they are the normal difficulties, fluctuations and struggles which come across the path of spiritual effort.[88]

SRI AUROBINDO

## 2. Difficulties – A Help for Realisation

Difficulties are sent to us exclusively to make the realisation more perfect.

Each time we try to realise something and meet with a resistance or an obstacle or even a failure – what seems to be a failure – we should know, we should never forget that it is exclusively, absolutely, so that the realisation may be more perfect.

So this habit of cringing, of getting discouraged or even of feeling uncomfortable, or of abusing yourself and telling yourself: "There! again I have made a mistake" – all that is absolute foolishness.

Simply tell yourself: "We don't know how to do things as they ought to be done; well, they are being done for us, come what may!" And if we could see to what extent all that seems to be, yes, a difficulty, a mistake, a failure, an obstacle – all that is just to help us, so that the realisation may be more perfect.

Once you know that, everything becomes easy.[89]

THE MOTHER

Shocks and trials always come as a divine grace to show us the points in our being where we fall short and the movements in which we turn our back on our soul by listening to the clamour of our mental being and vital being.

If we know how to accept these spiritual blows with due humility, we are sure to cover a great distance at a single bound.[90]

THE MOTHER

Be absolutely convinced that everything that happens, happens in order to give us precisely the lesson we needed, and if we are sincere in the "sadhana", the lesson should be accepted with joy and gratitude.

For one who aspires to the divine life, what can the actions of a blind and ignorant humanity matter to him?[91]

THE MOTHER

Difficulties are always blessings if we know how to face them.[92]

THE MOTHER

> *With the touch of the divine Grace, how do difficulties become opportunities for progress?*

... Well, this is something quite obvious. You have made a big mistake, you are in great difficulty: then, if you have faith, if you have trust in the divine Grace, if you really rely on It, you will suddenly realise that it is a lesson, that your difficulty or mistake is nothing else but a lesson and that it comes to teach you to find within yourself what needs to be changed, and with this help of the divine Grace you will discover in yourself what has to be changed. And you will change it. And so, from a difficulty you will have made great progress, taken a considerable leap forward. This, indeed, happens all the time. Only, you must be truly sincere, that is, rely on the Grace and let It work in you – not like this: one part of you asking to be helped and another resisting as much as it can, because it doesn't want to change....[93]

THE MOTHER

The difficulties are for the strong, and help to make them stronger.

Persevere and you will conquer.[94]

THE MOTHER

Difficulties come because there are possibilities in you. If in life everything was easy, then it would be a life of nothing. Because difficulties come on your way it shows you have possibilities.[95]

THE MOTHER

For the aspirant and the "sadhak", all that comes in his life comes to help him to know the Truth and to live it.[96]

THE MOTHER

The difficulties come always to make us progress. The greater the difficulty, the greater can be the progress.[97]

THE MOTHER

### 3. Difficulties of the Character

The difficulties of the character persist so long as one yields to them in action when they rise. One has to make a strict rule not to act according to the impulses of anger, ego or whatever the weakness may be that one wants to get rid of, or if one does act in the heat of the moment, not to justify or persist in the action. If one does that, after a time the difficulty abates or is confined purely to a subjective movement which one can observe, detach oneself from and combat.[98]

SRI AUROBINDO

... even the most beautiful theories, even if one knows mentally many things and holds admirable principles, that is not sufficiently strong to create a will capable of resisting an impulse. At one time you are quite determined, you have decided that it would be thus – for example, that you would not do such a thing: it is settled, you will not do it – but how is it that suddenly (you do not know how or why nor what has happened), you have not decided anything at all! And then you immediately find in yourself an excellent reason for doing the thing.... Among others, there is a certain kind of excuse which is always given: "Well, if I do it this time, at least I shall be convinced that it is very bad and I shall do it no longer and this will be the last time." It is the prettiest excuse one always gives to oneself: "This is the last time I am doing it. This time, I am doing it to understand perfectly that it is bad and that it must not be done and I shall not do it any more. This is the last time." Every time, it is the last time! and you begin again.

Of course there are some who have less clear ideas and who say to themselves: "After all, why don't I want to do it? These are theories, they are principles that might not be true. If I have this impulse, what is it that tells me that this impulse is not better than a theory?..." It is not for them the last time. It is something they accept as quite natural.

Between these two extremes there are all the possibilities. But the most dangerous of all is to say: "Well, I am doing it once more this time, that will purify me of this. Afterwards I shall no longer do it." Now the purification is never enough!

It happens only when you have decided: "Well, this

time, I am going to try not to do it, and I shall not do it, I shall apply all my strength and I shall not do it." Even if you have just a little success, it is much. Not a big success, but just a small success, a very partial success: you do not carry out what you yearn to do; but the yearning, the desire, the passion is still there and that produces whirls within, but outside you resist, "I shall not do it, I shall not move; even if I have to bind myself hand and foot, I shall not do it." It is a partial success – but it is a great victory because, due to this, next time you will be able to do a little more. That is to say, instead of holding all the violent passions within yourself, you can begin calming them a little; and you will calm them slowly at first, with difficulty. They will remain long, they will come back, they will trouble you, vex you, produce in you a great disgust, all that, but if you resist well and say: "No, I shall carry out nothing; whatever the cost, I shall not carry out anything; I will stay like a rock", then little by little, little by little, that thins out, thins out and you begin to learn the second attitude: "Now I want my consciousness to be above those things. There will still be many battles but if my consciousness stands above that, little by little there will come a time when this will return no longer." And then there is a time when you feel that you are absolutely free: you do not even perceive it, and then that is all. It may take a long time, it may come soon: that depends on the strength of character, on the sincerity of the aspiration. But even for people who have just a little sincerity, if they subject themselves to this process, they succeed. It takes time. They succeed in the first item: in not expressing. All forces upon earth tend towards expressing themselves. These forces come with the object of manifesting themselves and if you place a barrier and refuse expression, they may try to beat against the barrier for a time, but in the end, they will tire themselves out and not being manifested, they will withdraw and leave you quiet.

So you must never say: "I shall first purify my thought, purify my body, purify my vital and then later I shall purify my action." That is the normal order, but it never succeeds. The effective order is to begin from the outside: "The very first thing is that I do not do it, and afterwards, I desire it no longer and next I close my doors completely to all impulses: they no longer exist for me, I am now outside all that." This is the true order, the order that is effective. First, not to do it. And then you will no longer desire and after that it will go out of your consciousness completely.[99]

THE MOTHER

*Mother, there are mistakes... one knows they are mistakes, but still it is as though one were pushed into making them. Then?*

Pushed by what? Ah, this is exactly what happens! It is the lower nature, the instincts of the subconscient which govern you and make you do things you should not do. And so it is a choice between your will and accepting submission. There is always a moment when one can decide. It goes to the point where... there is even a moment when one can decide to be ill or not to be ill. It even goes so far that a moment comes when one can decide to die or not to die. But for that one must have an *extremely* awakened consciousness because this speck is infinitesimal in time and like the hundredth part of a second, and because before it one can do nothing and after it one can do nothing; but at that moment one can. And if one is absolutely awake, one can, at that moment, take the decision.

But for ordinary things, as for example, giving way before an impulse or refusing it, it is not a space, not even the space of a second; one has plenty of time before him, one certainly has several minutes. And it is a choice between weak submission and a controlling will. And if the will is clear, if it is based on truth, if truly it obeys the truth and is clear, it always has the power to refuse the wrong movement. It is an excuse you give yourself when you say, "I could not." It is not true. It is that truly you have not wanted it in the right way. For there is always the choice between saying "yes" and saying "no". But one chooses to be weak and later gives oneself this excuse, saying, "It is not my fault; it was stronger than I." It is your fault if the thing was stronger than you. Because you are not these impulses, you are a conscious soul and an intelligent will, and your duty is to see that *this* is what governs you and not the impulses from below.[100]

THE MOTHER

... there is one part of the being which has an aspiration, there is one part of the being which gives itself, and there are other parts – sometimes a small part, sometimes a big one which hides nicely, right at the bottom, and keeps absolutely quiet so that it may not be found out, but which *resists* with *all* its might, so as not to change....

... hidden somewhere there is a tiny something which is

well coiled up, in there, *doubled up, turned in* upon itself
and well hidden, right at the bottom, as at the bottom of a
box, which refuses to stir. (*Mother speaks very softly.*) So
when the effort, the aspiration wane, die down, this
springs up like that, gently, and then it wants to impose its
will and it makes you do exactly what you did not want to
do, what you had decided you would not do, and which
you do without knowing how or why! Because that thing
was there, it had its turn – for small things, big things, for
the details, even for the direction of life.

There are people who see clearly, who know so well
what they ought to do, and who feel that they can't....
They don't know why. It is nothing else but that. There is
a little spot which doesn't want to change and this little
spot awaits its hour. And the day it is allowed, through
laxity, fatigue, somnolence, through a little inertia, allowed to show itself, it will show itself with all concentrated, accumulated energy, and will make you do, will
make you say, make you feel, make you act *ex-act-ly*
contrary to what you had decided to do! And you will
stand there: "Ah, how discouraging this is!..." Then some
people say, "Fate!" They think it is their fate. It is not
fate, it is themselves!... It is that they don't have, haven't
used, the light, the searchlight. They have not turned the
searchlight into the small hidden corners of their being,
they haven't discovered what was well hidden. They have
left it there, and then have done this (*Mother turns away
her head*) so as not to see it. How many times one
suddenly feels one is on the point of catching something,
"Hup!" It hurts a little.... It is troublesome.... So one
thinks of something else, and that's all! The opportunity
has gone. One must wait for another occasion, again com-

mit a few stupidities, before being able to find an opportunity to catch the thing by the tail, like this, or by the ear or the nose, and hold it firmly and say, "No! you won't hide any longer now, I see you as you are, and you must either get out or change!"[101]

THE MOTHER

> *Mother, last time you said that often there is in us a dark element... which makes us commit stupidities. So you said that when one is conscious of this element, it must be pulled out. But does pulling it out mean... For example, when one is conscious that this element comes to make us do stupid things, then, if by an effort of will one abstains from doing it, can one say that one has pulled it out?...*

One has sat upon it.

> *Then, how to pull it out?*

For that, first of all, you must become conscious of it, you see, put it right in front of you, and cut the links which attach it to your consciousness. It is a work of inner psychology, you know.

One can see, when one studies oneself very attentively... you see that one day you are very generous... generous in your feelings, generous in your sensations, generous in your thoughts and even in material things; that is, you understand the faults of others, their intentions, weaknesses, even nasty movements. You see all this, and you are full of good feelings, of generosity. You tell yourself, "Well... everyone does the best he can!" – like that.

Another day – or perhaps the very next minute – you will notice in yourself a kind of dryness, fixity, something that is bitter, that judges severely, that goes as far as bearing a grudge, has rancour, would like the evil-doer punished, that almost has feelings of vengeance; just the very opposite of the former! One day someone harms you and you say, "Doesn't matter! He did not know"... or "He couldn't do otherwise"... or "That's his nature"... or "He could not understand!" The next day – or perhaps an hour later – you say, "He must be punished! He must pay for it! He must be made to feel that he has done wrong!" – with a kind of rage; and you want to take things, you want to keep them for yourself, you have all the feelings of jealousy, envy, narrowness, you see, just the very opposite of the other feeling.

This is the dark side. And so, the moment one sees it, if one looks at it and doesn't say, "It is I", if one says, "No, it is my shadow, it is the being I must throw out of myself", one puts on it the light of the other part, one tries to bring them face to face; and with the knowledge and light of the other, one doesn't try so much to convince – because that is very difficult – but one compels it to remain quiet... first to stand farther away, then one flings it very far away so that it can no longer return – putting a great light on it. There are instances in which it is possible to change, but this is very rare. There are instances in which one can put upon this being – or this shadow – put upon it such an intense light that it transforms it, and it changes into what is the truth of your being.

But this is a rare thing.... It can be done, but it is rare.

Usually, the best thing is to say, "No, this is not I! I don't want it! I have nothing to do with this movement, it doesn't exist for me, it is something contrary to my nature!" And so, by dint of insisting and driving it away, finally one separates oneself from it.

But one must first be clear and sincere enough to see the conflict within oneself. Usually one doesn't pay any attention to these things. One goes from one extreme to the other. You see, you can say, to put it in very simple words: one day I am good, the next day I am bad. And this seems quite natural.... Or even, sometimes for one hour you are good and the next hour you are wicked; or else, sometimes the whole day through one is good and suddenly one becomes wicked, for a minute very wicked, all the more wicked as one was good! Only, one doesn't observe it, thoughts cross one's mind, violent, bad, hateful things, like that.... Usually one pays no attention to it. But this is what must be caught! As soon as it manifests, you must catch it like this (*Mother makes a movement*) with a very firm grip, and then hold it, hold it up to the light and say, "No! I don't want you! I – don't – want – you! I have nothing to do with this! You are going to get out of here, and you won't return!"

(*After a silence*) And this is something – an experience that one can have daily, or almost... when one has those movements of great enthusiasm, great aspiration, when one suddenly becomes conscious of the divine goal, the urge towards the Divine, the desire to take part in the divine work, when one comes out of oneself in a great joy and great force... and then, a few hours later, one is miserable for a tiny little thing; one indulges in so petty, so narrow, so commonplace a self-interestedness, has such a dull desire... and all the rest has evaporated as if it did not exist. One is quite accustomed to contradictions; one doesn't pay attention to this and that is why all these things live comfortably together as neigbours. One must first discover them and prevent them from intermingling in one's consciousness: decide between them, separate the shadow from the light. Later one can get rid of the shadow.[102]

THE MOTHER

Seekers are always told, "If you want to get rid of something, say that it is outside." This is only an impression, but it is easier to get rid of a difficulty if you have the impression that it is outside you... what is inside is also outside and what is outside is also inside! The secret lies in knowing how to place it just where it is most convenient for the immediate action.

If you have a serious difficulty in your character, for example, the habit of losing your temper, and you decide: "I must not get angry again", it is very difficult, but if on the other hand, you tell yourself: "Anger is something which circulates through the whole world, it is not in me, it belongs to everybody; it wanders about here and there and if I close my door, it will not enter", it is much more easy. If you think: "It is my character, I am born like that", it becomes almost impossible. It is true there is something in your character which answers to this force of anger. All movements, all vibrations are general – they enter, they go out, they move about – but they rush upon you and enter into you only to the extent you leave the door in you open. And if you have, besides, some affinity with these forces, you may get angry without even knowing why.[103]

THE MOTHER

*"The first effect of Yoga, however, is to take away the mental control, and the hungers that lie dormant are suddenly set free; they rush up and invade the being.... What you should do is to keep the thing away from you, to disassociate from it, take as little notice of it as possible and, even if you happen to think of it, to remain indifferent and unconcerned."*

THE MOTHER
*Questions and Answers 1929*

This is much more difficult than to sit upon a difficulty! It is much more difficult to stand back from the difficulty, [than to sit upon it] to look at it as something which does not concern you, which does not interest you, does not belong to you, which belongs to the world and not to you – but it is only by doing this that you can succeed. This demands a kind of liberation of spirit and a confidence in your inner being: you must believe that if you take the right attitude, it is the best that will happen to you; but if you are afraid when something unpleasant happens to you, then you can do nothing. You must have this confidence within you, whatever the difficulty, whatever the obstacle. Most of the time, when something unpleasant happens, you say, "Is it going to increase? What other accident is yet going to happen!" and so on. You must tell yourself, "These things are not mine; they belong to the subconscious world; to be sure I have nothing to do with them and if they come again to seize me, I am going to give a fight." Naturally you will answer that this is easy to say but difficult to do. But if truly you take this attitude of confidence, there is no difficulty that you will not be able to conquer. Anxiety makes the difficulty greater.

Evidently there is one difficulty; in your conscious being something does not want the difficulty, wishes sincerely to overcome it, but there are numberless movements in other parts of your consciousness of which you are not conscious. You say, "I want to be cured of that"; unfortunately it is not sufficient to say "I want", there are other parts of the consciousness which hide themselves so that you may not be busy with them, and when your attention is turned away these parts try to assert themselves. That is why I say and shall always repeat, Be perfectly sincere; do not try to deceive yourself, do not say, "I have done all that I could". If you do not succeed, it means that you do not do all that you can. For, if you truly do "all" that you can, you will surely succeed. If you have any defect which you want to get rid of and which still persists, and you say, "I have done all that I could", you may be sure that you have not done all that you should have. If you had, you would have triumphed, for the difficulties that come to you are exactly in proportion to your strength – nothing can happen to you which does not belong to your consciousness, and all that belongs to your consciousness you are able to master. Even the things and suggestions that come from outside can touch you only in proportion to the consent of your consciousness, and you are made to be the master of your consciousness. If you say, "I have done all that I could and in spite of everything the thing continues, so I give up", you may be already sure that you have not done what you could. When an error persists "in spite of everything" it means that something hidden in your being springs up suddenly like a Jack-in-the-box and takes the helm of your life. Hence, there is only one thing to do, it is to go hunting for all the little dark corners which lie hidden in you and, if you put just a tiny spark of goodwill on this darkness, it will yield, will vanish, and what appeared to you impossible will become not only possible, practicable, but *it will have been done*. You can in this way in one minute get rid of a difficulty which would have harassed you for years. I absolutely assure you of it. That depends only on one thing: that you truly, sincerely, want to get rid of it. And it is the same for everything, from physical illnesses up to the highest mental difficulties. One part of the consciousness says, "I don't want it", but behind there hides a heap of things which say nothing, do not show themselves, and which just want that things continue as they are – generally out of ignorance; they do not believe that it is necessary to be cured, they believe that everything is for the best in the best of worlds.[104]

THE MOTHER

And finally, lest you get discouraged by your own faults, the Dhammapada gives you this solacing image: the purest lily can spring out of a heap of rubbish by the wayside. That is to say, there is nothing so rotten that it cannot give birth to the purest realisation.

Whatever may be the past, whatever may be the faults committed, whatever the ignorance in which one might have lived, one carries deep within oneself the supreme

purity which can translate itself into a wonderful realisation.

The whole point is to think of that, to concentrate on
that and not to be concerned with all the difficulties and
obstacles and hindrances.

Concentrate exclusively on what you want to be, forget
as entirely as possible what you do not want to be.[105]

THE MOTHER

## 4. Universal Adverse Forces

... the prolongation of the difficulty and its acuteness
come from the fact that there are Forces in Nature, not
personal or individual but universal, which live upon these
movements and through them have long controlled the
individual nature. These do not want to lose their rule and
so when these movements are thrown out, they throw
them back on the sadhak in strong waves or with great
violence. Or they create in the vital a great depression,
discouragement, despair – that is their favourite weapon
– because it is losing its former field of desires and has not
yet in any certainty something that would replace it, the
assured continuous psychic or spiritual condition or experience. To prevent that is the whole effort of these Forces.
So they create these upheavals and the vital admits them
because of its own habit of response to the lower Forces.
At the same time they put in suggestions to the mind so as
to make it also accept the disturbance, discouragement
and depression. That is what I meant by saying that these
are attacks from outside and must be rejected. If they
cannot be rejected altogether, yet one must try to keep a

part of the mind conscious which will refuse to admit the suggestions or share in the depression and the trouble, – which will say firmly "I know what this is and I know that it will pass and I can resume my way to the goal which nothing can prevent me from reaching, since my soul's will is and will always be for that." You have to reach the point where you can do that always; then the power of the Forces to disturb will begin to diminish and fall away.[106]

SRI AUROBINDO

*How is one to meet adverse forces – forces that are invisible and yet quite living and tangible?*

A great deal depends upon the stage of development of your consciousness. At the beginning, if you have no special occult knowledge and power, the best you can do is to keep as quiet and peaceful as possible. If the attack takes the form of adverse suggestions try quietly to push them away, as you would some material object. The quieter you are, the stronger you become. The firm basis of all spiritual power is equanimity. You must not allow anything to disturb your poise: you can then resist every kind of attack. If, besides, you possess sufficient discernment and can see and catch the evil suggestions as they come to you, it becomes all the more easy for you to push them away; but sometimes they come unnoticed, and then it is more difficult to fight them. When that happens, you must sit quiet and call down peace and a deep inner quietness. Hold yourself firm and call with confidence and faith: if your aspiration is pure and steady, you are sure to receive help.

Attacks from adverse forces are inevitable: you have to
take them as tests on your way and go courageously
through the ordeal. The struggle may be hard, but when
you come out of it you have gained something, you have
advanced a step. There is even a necessity for the existence of the hostile forces. They make your determination
stronger, your aspiration clearer.

It is true, however, that they exist because you gave
them reason to exist. So long as there is something in you
which answers to them, their intervention is perfectly
legitimate. If nothing in you responded, if they had no
hold upon any part of your nature, they would retire and
leave you. In any case, they need not stop or hamper your
spiritual progress.

The only way to fail in your battle with the hostile forces
is not to have a true confidence in the divine help.
Sincerity in the aspiration always brings down the re-
quired succour. A quiet call, a conviction that in this
ascension towards the realisation you are never walking
all alone and a faith that whenever help is needed it is
there, will lead you through easily and securely.[107]

THE MOTHER

*Do these hostile forces generally come from outside
or inside?*

If you think or feel that they come from inside, you have
possibly opened yourself to them and they have settled in
you unnoticed. The true nature of things is one of
harmony; but there is a distortion in certain worlds that

brings in perversion and hostility. If you have a strong affinity for these worlds of distortion, you can become friends with the beings that are there and answer fully to them. That happens, but it is not a very happy condition. The consciousness is at once blinded and you cannot distinguish the true from the false, you cannot even tell what is a lie and what is not.

In any case, when an attack comes the wisest attitude is to consider that it comes from outside and to say, "This is not myself and I will have nothing to do with it." You have to deal in the same way with all lower impulses and desires and all doubts and questionings in the mind. If you identify yourself with them, the difficulty in fighting them becomes all the greater; for then you have the feeling that you are facing the never easy task of overcoming your own nature. But once you are able to say, "No, this is not myself, I will have nothing to do with it", it becomes much easier to disperse them.[108]

THE MOTHER

## 5. Discouragement and Depression

All who enter the spiritual path have to face the difficulties and ordeals of the path, those which rise from their own nature and those which come in from outside. The difficulties in the nature always rise again and again till you overcome them; they must be faced with both strength and patience. But the vital part is prone to depression when ordeals and difficulties rise. This is not peculiar to you, but comes to all sadhaks – it does not imply an unfitness for the sadhana or justify a sense of helplessness. But you must train yourself to overcome this reaction of depression....

All who cleave to the path steadfastly can be sure of their spiritual destiny. If anyone fails to reach it, it can only be for one of the two reasons, either because they leave the path or because for some lure of ambition, vanity, desire, etc. they go astray from the sincere dependence on the Divine.[109]

SRI AUROBINDO

Do not allow any discouragement to come upon you and have no distrust of the Divine Grace. Whatever difficulties are outside you, whatever weaknesses are inside you, if you keep firm hold on your faith and your aspiration, the secret Power will carry you through.... Even if you are oppressed with opposition and difficulties, even if you stumble, even if the way seems closed to you, keep hold on your aspiration... keep firm on the way – then in the end things open out of themselves and circumstances yield to the inner spirit.[110]

SRI AUROBINDO

Depression is a sign of weakness, of a bad will somewhere, and bad will in the sense of a refusal to receive help, and a kind of weakness that's content to be weak. One becomes slack. The bad will is obvious, because there's a part of your being which tells you at that moment, "Depression is bad." You know that you shouldn't get depressed; well, the reply of that part which

is depressed is almost, "Shut up! I want my depression."
Try, you will see, you can try. It is always like that.... And
then later one says again, "Afterwards, afterwards I shall
see... for the moment I want it, and besides I have my
reasons." There you are. It is a kind of revolt, a weak
revolt, the revolt of something weak in the being.

... When one comes out of the depression and one's bad
will, well, then one realises that there was an attack and
that some progress had to be made, and that in spite of
everything something within has made progress, that one
has taken a step forward. Usually, hardly consciously, it is
something which needs to progress but doesn't want to,
and so takes this way; like a child who sulks, becomes low-
spirited, sad, unhappy, misunderstood, abandoned, help-
less; and then, refusing to collaborate, and as I just said,
indulging in his depression, to show that he is not happy.
It is specially in order to show that one is not satisfied that
one becomes depressed. One can show it to Nature, one
can show it (that depends on the case, you see), one can
show it to the Divine, one can show it to the people
around one, but it is always a kind of way of expressing
one's dissatisfaction. "I am not happy about what you
demand", but this means, "I am not happy. And I shall
make you too see it, that I am not happy."...

But when it is over, and when for some reason or other
one has made the necessary effort to come out of it, and
has come out, one usually realises that something in the
being has changed, because, in spite of all bad will, most
often the progress was accomplished – not very swiftly,
not very brilliantly, not for one's greater glory, surely, but
still the progress was made. Something has changed.[111]

THE MOTHER

Why do you indulge in these exaggerated feelings of remorse and despair when these things come up from the subconscient? They do not help and make it more, not less, difficult to eliminate what comes. Such returns of an old nature that is long expelled from the conscious parts of the being always happen in sadhana. It does not at all mean that the nature is unchangeable. Try to recover the inner quietude, draw back from these movements and look at them calmly, reducing them to their true proportions. Your true nature is that in which you have peace and Ananda and love of the Divine. This other is only a fringe of the outer personality which in spite of these returns is destined to drop away as the true being extends and increases.[112]

Sri Aurobindo

There is no reason to be so much cut down or despair of your progress. Evidently, you have had a surging up of the old movements, but that can always happen so long as there is not an entire change of the old nature both in the consciousness and subconscient parts.... The one thing to do is to quiet yourself and get back into the true consciousness and poise.[113]

Sri Aurobindo

Do not allow yourself to admit any movement of vital depression, still less a depressed condition. As for the external being, it is always, not only in you but in everyone, a difficult animal to handle. It has to be dealt with by patience and a quiet and cheerful perseverance; never get depressed by its resistance, for that only makes it sensitive and aggrieved and difficult, or else discouraged. Give it rather the encouragement of sunlight and a quiet pressure, and one day you will find it opening entirely to the Grace.[114]

SRI AUROBINDO

One must learn to go forward on the path of yoga, as the Gita insists, with a consciousness free from despondency – *anirviṇṇacetasā*. Even if one slips, one must rectify the posture; even if one falls, one has to rise and go undiscouraged on the Divine Way. The attitude must be:

"The Divine has promised Himself to me if I cleave to Him always; that I will never cease to do whatever may come."[115]

SRI AUROBINDO

... the great need in all crises and attacks, – to refuse to listen to any suggestions, impulses, lures and to oppose to them all the call of the Truth, the imperative beckoning of the Light. In all doubt and depression, to say, "I belong to the Divine, I cannot fail"; to all suggestions of impurity and unfitness, to reply, "I am a child of Immortality chosen by the Divine; I have but to be true to myself and to Him – the victory is sure; even if I fell, I would rise again"; to all impulses to... serve some smaller ideal, to reply, "This is the greatest, this is the Truth that alone can satisfy the soul within me; I will endure through all tests

and tribulations to the very end of the divine journey".
This is what I mean by faithfulness to the Light and the
Call.[116]

SRI AUROBINDO

Difficulty cannot be overcome by your running away from
it.

... It is not by tormenting yourself with remorse and
harassing thoughts that you can overcome. It is by looking
straight at yourself, very quietly, with a quiet and firm
resolution and then going on cheerfully and bravely in full
confidence and reliance, trusting in the Grace, serenely
and vigilantly, anchoring yourself on your psychic
being.... That is the true way – and there is no other.[117]

SRI AUROBINDO

... to keep steady one's aspiration and to look at oneself
with an absolute sincerity are the sure means to overcome
all obstacles.[118]

THE MOTHER

## 6. Worry and Perplexity

Let us live each day without anxiety. Why worry beforehand about something that will probably never happen?[119]

THE MOTHER

Don't foresee difficulties – it does not help to surmount them and helps them to come.[120]

THE MOTHER

Live in the consciousness of the Eternal and you will have no more worry.[121]

THE MOTHER

... if at a particular moment there is something which holds you, grips you like that, holds you tight, close pressed, and you absolutely want it to happen, and you are fighting against a terrible obstacle, you see, something which is preventing it from happening; if simply just at that moment you begin to feel, to realise the myriads and myriads of years there were before this present moment, and the myriads and myriads of years there will be after this present moment, and what importance this little event has in relation to all that – there is no need to enter a spiritual consciousness or anything else, simply enter into relation with space and time, with all that is before, all that is after and all that is happening at the same time – if one is not an idiot, immediately he tells himself, "Oh, well, I am attaching importance to something which doesn't have any." Necessarily so, you see. It loses all its importance, immediately.

If you can visualise, you know, simply the immensity of the creation – I am not now speaking of rising to spiritual heights – simply the immensity of the creation in time and space, and this little event on which you are concentrated with an importance... as though it were something of some importance... immediately it does this (*gesture*) and it dissolves, if you do it sincerely. If, naturally, there is one part of yourself which tells you, "Ah, but for me it has an importance", then, there, you have only to leave that part behind and keep your consciousness as it is. But if sincerely you want to see the true value of things, it is very easy.

There are other methods, you know. There is a Chinese sage who advises you to lie down upon events as one floats on one's back upon the sea, imagining the immensity of the ocean and that you let yourself go floating upon this... upon the waves, you see, like something contemplating the skies and letting itself be carried away. In Chinese they call this *Wu Weï*. When you can do this all your troubles are gone. I knew an Irishman who used to lie flat on his back and look outside, as much as possible on an evening when stars were in the sky, he looked, contemplated the sky and imagined that he was floating in that immensity of countless luminous points.

And immediately all troubles are calmed.

There are many ways. But sincerely, you have only to... have the sense of relativity between your little person and the importance you give to the things which concern you, and the universal immensity; this is enough. Naturally, there is another way, it is to free oneself from the earth consciousness and rise into a higher consciousness where these terrestrial things take their true place – which is quite small, you see.[122]

THE MOTHER

It is an inexpressible joy not to have any responsibility for oneself, no longer to think of oneself. It is so dull and monotonous and insipid to be thinking of oneself, to be worrying about what to do and what not to do, what will be good for you and what will be bad for you, what to shun and what to pursue – oh, how wearisome it is! But when one lives like this, quite open, like a flower blossoming in the sun before the Supreme Consciousness, the Supreme Wisdom, the Supreme Light, the Supreme Love, which knows all, which can do all, which takes charge of you and you have no more worries – that is the ideal condition.

And why is it not done?

One does not think of it, one forgets to do it, the old habits come back. And above all, behind, hidden somewhere in the inconscient or even in the subconscient, there is this insidious doubt that whispers in your ear: "Oh! if you are not careful, some misfortune will happen to you. If you forget to watch over yourself, you do not know what may happen" – and you are so silly, so silly, so obscure, so stupid that you listen and you begin to pay attention to yourself and everything is ruined.

You have to begin all over again to infuse into your cells a little wisdom, a little common sense and learn once more not to worry.[123]

THE MOTHER

Difficulties and perplexities can never be got rid of by the mind brooding on them and trying in that way to get out of them; this habit of the mind only makes them recur without a solution and keeps up by brooding the persistent tangle. It is from something above and outside the perplexities that the solution must come. The difficulty of the physical mind – not the true thinking intelligence – is that it does not want to believe in this larger consciousness outside itself because it is not aware of it; and it remains shut like a box in itself, not admitting the light that is all round it and pressing to get in. It is a subtle law of the action of consciousness that if you stress difficulties – you have to observe them, of course, but not stress them, they will quite sufficiently do that for themselves – the difficulties tend to stick or even increase; on the contrary, if you put your whole stress on faith and aspiration and concentrate steadily on what you aspire to, that will sooner or later tend towards realisation. It is this change of stress, a change in the poise and attitude of the mind, that will be the more helpful process.[124]

SRI AUROBINDO

The noise made by all the words, all the ideas in your head is so deafening that it prevents you from hearing the truth when it wants to manifest.

To learn to be quiet and silent... When you have a problem to solve, instead of turning over in your head all the possibilities, all the consequences, all the possible things one should or should not do, if you remain quiet with an aspiration for goodwill, if possible a need for goodwill, the solution comes very quickly. And as you are silent you are able to hear it.

When you are caught in a difficulty, try this method: instead of becoming agitated, turning over all the ideas and actively seeking solutions, of worrying, fretting, running here and there inside your head... *remain quiet*.

And according to your nature, with ardour or peace, with intensity or widening or with all these together, implore the Light and wait for it to come.

In this way the path would be considerably shortened.[125]

THE MOTHER

## 7. Dryness and Arrest of Progress

... the interval periods when all is quiet and nothing being done on the surface... come to all and cannot be avoided. You must not cherish the suggestion that it is because of your want of aspiration or any other unfitness that it is so and, if you had the constant ardent aspiration, then there would be no such periods and there would be an uninter-rupted stream of experiences. It is not so. Even if the aspiration were there, the interval periods would come. If even in them one can aspire, so much the better – but the main thing is to meet them with quietude and not become restless, depressed or despondent. A constant fire can be there only when a certain stage has been reached, that is when one is always inside consciously living in the psychic being, but for that all this preparation of the mind, vital, physical is necessary. For this fire belongs to the psychic and one cannot command it always merely by the mind's effort.[126]

SRI AUROBINDO

Naturally, the more one-pointed the aspiration the swifter the progress. The difficulty comes when either the vital with its desires or the physical with its past habitual movements comes in – as they do with almost everyone. It is then that the dryness and difficulty of spontaneous aspiration come. This dryness is a well-known obstacle in all sadhana. But one has to persist and not be discouraged. If one keeps the will fixed even in these barren periods, they pass and after their passage a greater force of aspiration and experience becomes possible.[127]

SRI AUROBINDO

The physical consciousness is always in everybody in its own nature a little inert and in it a constant strong aspiration is not natural, it has to be created. But first there must be the opening, a purification, a fixed quietude, otherwise the physical vital will turn the strong aspiration into over-eagerness and impatience or rather it will try to give it that turn. Do not therefore be troubled if the state of the nature seems to you to be too neutral and quiet, not enough aspiration and movement in it. This is a passage necessary for the progress and the rest will come.[128]

SRI AUROBINDO

A difficulty comes or an arrest in some movement which you have begun or have been carrying on for some time. How is it to be dealt with – for such arrests are inevitably frequent enough, not only for you, but for everyone who is a seeker; one might almost say that every step forward is followed by an arrest – at least, that is a very common, if not a universal experience. It is to be dealt with by becoming always more quiet, more firm in the will to go through, by opening oneself more and more so that any obstructing non-receptivity in the nature may diminish or disappear, by an affirmation of faith even in the midst of the obscurity, faith in the presence of a Power that is working behind the cloud and the veil, in the guidance of the Guru, by an observation of oneself to find any cause of the arrest, not in a spirit of depression or discouragement but with the will to find out and remove it. This is the only right attitude and, if one is persistent in taking it, the periods of arrest are not abolished, – for that cannot be at this stage, – but greatly shortened and lightened in their incidence. Sometimes these arrests are periods, long or short, of assimilation or unseen preparation, their appearance of sterile immobility is deceptive: in that case, with the right attitude, one can after a time, by opening, by observation, by accumulated experience, begin to feel, to get some inkling of what is being prepared or done. Sometimes it is a period of true obstruction in which the Power at work has to deal with the obstacles in the way, obstacles in oneself, obstacles of the opposing cosmic forces or any other or of all together, and this kind of arrest may be long or short according to the magnitude or obstinacy or complexity of the impediments that are met. But here, too, the right attitude can alleviate or shorten and, if persistently taken, help to a more radical removal of the difficulties and greatly diminish the necessity of complete arrests hereafter.

On the contrary, an attitude of depression or unfaith in the help or the guidance or in the certitude of the victory of the guiding Power, a shutting up of yourself in the sense of the difficulties impedes the recovery, prolongs the difficulties, helps the obstructions to recur with force instead of progressively diminishing in their incidence. It is an attitude whose persistence or recurrence you must resolutely throw aside if you want to get over the obstruction which you feel so much – which the depressed attitude only makes, while it lasts, more acute.[129]

SRI AUROBINDO

## 8. Illness and Suffering

The feeling of illness is at first only a suggestion; it becomes a reality because your physical consciousness accepts it. It is like a wrong suggestion in the mind, – if the mind accepts it, it becomes clouded and confused and has to struggle back into harmony and clearness. It is so with the body consciousness and illness. You must not accept but reject it with your physical mind and so help the body consciousness to throw off the suggestion. If necessary, make a counter-suggestion "No, I shall be well; I am and shall be all right."[130]

SRI AUROBINDO

By will to illness I meant this that there is something in the body that accepts the illness and has certain reactions that make this acceptance effective – so there must always be a contrary will in the conscious parts of the being to get rid of this most physical acceptance.[131]

SRI AUROBINDO

What I meant was that the body consciousness through old habit of consciousness admits the force of illness and goes through the experiences which are associated with it – e.g., congestion of phlegm in the chest and feeling of suffocation or difficulty of breathing, etc. To get rid of that one must awaken a will and consciousness in the body itself that refuses to allow these things to impose themselves upon it. But to get that, still more to get it completely is difficult. One step towards it is to get the inner consciousness separate from the body – to feel that it is not you who are ill, but it is only something taking place in the body and affecting your consciousness. It is then possible to see this separate body consciousness, what it feels, what are its reactions to things, how it works. One can then act on it to change its consciousness and reactions.[132]

SRI AUROBINDO

Certainly, one can act from within on an illness and cure it. Only it is not always easy as there is much resistance in Matter, a resistance of inertia. An untiring persistence is necessary; at first one may fail altogether or the symptoms increase, but gradually the control of the body or of a particular illness becomes stronger. Again, to cure an occasional attack of illness by inner means is comparatively easy, to make the body immune from it in future is more difficult. A chronic malady is harder to deal with, more reluctant to disappear entirely than an occasional disturbance of the body. So long as the control of the body is imperfect, there are all these and other imperfections and difficulties in the use of the inner force.

If you can succeed by the inner action in preventing increase, even that is something; you have then by *abhyāsa* to strengthen the power till it becomes able to cure. Note that so long as the power is not entirely there, some aid of physical means need not be altogether rejected.[133]

SRI AUROBINDO

Above all, do not harbour that idea of an unfit body – all suggestions of that kind are a subtle attack on the will to siddhi and especially dangerous in physical matters... the first business is to expel it bag and baggage. Appearances and facts may be all in its favour, but the first condition of success for the yogin and indeed for anybody who wants to do anything great or unusual is to be superior to facts and disbelieve in appearances. Will to be free from disease, however formidable, many-faced or constant its attacks, and repel all contrary suggestions.[134]

SRI AUROBINDO

To bear extreme heat and cold it is necessary to have peace in the cells first, then consolidated force. Pain and discomfort come from a physical consciousness not forceful enough to determine its own reactions to things.[135]

SRI AUROBINDO

The body, naturally [experiences physical pain] – but the body transmits it to the vital and mental. With the ordinary consciousness the vital gets disturbed and afflicted and its forces diminished, the mind identifies and is upset. The mind has to remain unmoved, the vital unaffected, and the body has to learn to take it with equality so that the higher Force may work.[136]

SRI AUROBINDO

The Self is never affected by any kind of pain. The psychic takes it quietly and offers it to the Divine for what is necessary to be done.[137]

SRI AUROBINDO

It is a detachment of even the physical mind from the pain that makes one able to go on as if nothing were there but this detachment of the physical mind is not so easy to acquire.[138]

SRI AUROBINDO

The main difficulty seems to be that you are too subject to an excitement of the nerves – it is only by bringing quietude and calm into the whole being that a steady progress in the sadhana can be assured.

The first thing to be done in order to recover is to stop yielding to the attack of the nerves – the more you yield and identify yourself with these ideas and feelings, the more they increase.[139]

SRI AUROBINDO

Suffering is not inflicted as a punishment for sin or for hostility – that is a wrong idea. Suffering comes like pleasure and good fortune as an inevitable part of life in the ignorance. The dualities of pleasure and pain, joy and grief, good fortune and ill-fortune are the inevitable results of the ignorance which separates us from our true consciousness and from the Divine. Only by coming back to it can we get rid of suffering. Karma from the past lives exists, much of what happens is due to it, but not all. For we can mend our karma by our own consciousness and efforts. But the suffering is simply a natural consequence of past errors, not a punishment, just as a burn is the natural consequence of playing with fire. It is part of the experience by which the soul through its instruments learns and grows until it is ready to turn to the Divine.[140]

SRI AUROBINDO

The attitude you express in your letter is quite the right one – whatever sufferings come on the path, are not too high a price for the victory that has to be won and if they are taken in the right spirit, they become even a means towards the victory.[141]

SRI AUROBINDO

# V

# ATTITUDES ON THE PATH

# ATTITUDES ON THE PATH

## 1. Quiet, Aspiration and Peace

To live within in a constant aspiration for the Divine enables us to look at life with a smile and to remain peaceful whatever the outer circumstances may be.[142]

THE MOTHER

Always seek to progress in quietude, happiness and confidence, that is the most helpful attitude. Do not listen to contrary suggestions from outside.[143]

SRI AUROBINDO

A simple, straight and sincere call and aspiration from the heart is the one important thing and more essential and effective than capacities. Also to get the consciousness to turn inwards, not remain outward-going is of great importance – to arrive at the inner call, the inner experience, the inner Presence.[144]

SRI AUROBINDO

The sattwic nature has always been held to be the most apt and ready for the spiritual life, while the rajasic nature is encumbered by its desires and passions. At the same time, spirituality is something above the dualities, and what is most needed for it is a true upward aspiration. This may come to the rajasic man as well as to the sattwic. If it does, he can rise by it above his failings and desires and

passions, just as the other can rise beyond his virtues, to
the Divine Purity and Light and Love.[145]

SRI AUROBINDO

Aspiration should be not a form of desire, but the feeling
of an inner soul's need, and a quiet settled will to turn
towards the Divine and seek the Divine. It is certainly not
easy to get rid of this mixture of desire entirely – not easy
for anyone; but when one has the will to do it, this also can
be effected by the help of the sustaining Force.[146]

SRI AUROBINDO

Desire often leads either to excess of effort, meaning
often much labour and a limited fruit with strain, exhaus-
tion and in case of difficulty or failure, despondence,
disbelief or revolt; or else it leads to pulling down the
force. That can be done, but except for the yogically
strong and experienced, it is not always safe, though it
may be often very effective; not safe, first, because it may
lead to violent reactions or it brings down contrary or
wrong or mixed forces which the sadhak is not experienced enough to distinguish from the true ones. Or else
it may substitute the sadhak's own limited power of
experience or his mental and vital constructions for the
free gift and true leading of the Divine.[147]

SRI AUROBINDO

The impatience and restless disquietude come from the
vital which brings that even into the aspiration. The

aspiration must be intense, calm and strong (that is the nature of the true vital also) and not restless and impatient, – then alone it can be stable.[148]

SRI AUROBINDO

There can be an intense but quiet aspiration which does not disturb the harmony of the inner being.[149]

SRI AUROBINDO

Calm, discrimination, detachment (but not indifference) are all very important, for their opposites impede very much the transforming action. Intensity of aspiration should be there, but it must go along with these. No hurry, no inertia, neither rajasic over-eagerness nor tamasic discouragement – a steady and persistent but quiet call and working.[150]

SRI AUROBINDO

To remain quiet within, firm in the will to go through, refusing to be disturbed or discouraged by difficulties or fluctuations, that is one of the first things to be learned in the Path. To do otherwise is to encourage the instability of consciousness....

A spiritual atmosphere is more important than outer conditions; if one can get that and also create one's own spiritual air to breathe in and live in it, that is the true condition of progress.[151]

SRI AUROBINDO

You should realise that while quiet surroundings are desirable, the true quiet is within and no other will give the condition you want.[152]

SRI AUROBINDO

Aspire, concentrate in the right spirit and, whatever the difficulties, you are sure to attain the aim you have put before you.

It is in the peace behind... that you must learn to live and feel it to be yourself. You must regard the rest as not your real self, but only a flux of changing or recurring movements on the surface which are sure to go as the true self emerges.

Peace is the true remedy; distraction by hard work is only a temporary relief – although a certain amount of work is necessary for the proper balance of the different parts of the being.[153]

SRI AUROBINDO

If you get peace, then to clean the vital becomes easy. If you simply clean and clean and do nothing else, you go very slowly – for the vital gets dirty again and has to be cleaned a hundred times. The peace is something that is clean in itself, so to get it is a positive way of securing your object. To look for dirt only and clean is the negative way.[154]

SRI AUROBINDO

## 2. Sincerity

Sincere is simply an adjective meaning that the will must be a true will. If you simply think "I aspire" and do things inconsistent with the aspiration, or follow your desires or open yourself to contrary influences, then it is not a sincere will.[155]

SRI AUROBINDO

It is true that a central sincerity is not enough except as a beginning and a base; the sincerity must spread... through the whole nature. But still unless there is a double nature (without a central harmonising consciousness), the basis is usually sufficient for that to happen.[156]

SRI AUROBINDO

You speak of insincerity in your nature. If insincerity means the unwillingness of some part of the being to live according to the highest light one has or to equate the outer with the inner man, then this part is always insincere in all. The only way is to lay stress on the inner being and develop in it the psychic and spiritual consciousness till that comes down in it which pushes out the darkness from the outer man also.[157]

SRI AUROBINDO

Men are always mixed and there are qualities and defects mingled together almost inextricably in their nature. What a man wants to be or wants others to see in him or what he is sometimes on one side of his nature or in some relations can be very different from what he is in the actual fact or in other relations or on another side of his nature. To be absolutely sincere, straightforward, open, is not an easy achievement for human nature. It is only by spiritual endeavour that one can realise it – and to do it needs a severity of introspective self-vision, an unsparing scrutiny of self-observation of which many sadhaks and yogis even are not capable and it is only by an illumining Grace that reveals the sadhak to himself and transforms what is deficient in him that it can be done. And even then only if he himself consents and lends himself wholly to the divine working.[158]

SRI AUROBINDO

*He who puts on the yellow robe while he is yet impure, lacking in self-control and lacking in loyalty, truly he is unworthy to wear the yellow robe of the monk.*

The Dhammapada

It is noteworthy that the two defects insisted upon here are lack of self-control and lack of loyalty. Loyalty means here sincerity, honesty; what the Dhammapada censures most severely is hypocrisy: to pretend that you want to live the spiritual life and not to do it, to pretend that you want to seek the truth and not to do it, to display the external signs of consecration to the divine life – here symbolised by the yellow robe – but within to be concerned only with oneself, one's selfishness and one's own needs.[159]

THE MOTHER

Fundamentally, whatever be the path one follows – whether the path of surrender, consecration, knowledge – if one wants it to be perfect, it is always equally difficult, and there is but one way, one only, I know of only one: that is perfect sincerity, but *perfect* sincerity!

Do you know what perfect sincerity is?...

Never to try to deceive oneself, never let any part of the being try to find out a way of convincing the others, never to explain favourably what one does in order to have an excuse for what one wants to do, never to close one's eyes when something is unpleasant, never to let anything pass, telling oneself, "That is not important, next time it will be better."

Oh! it is very difficult. Just try for one hour and you will see how very difficult it is. Only one hour, to be *totally, absolutely* sincere. To let nothing pass. That is, all one does, all one feels, all one thinks, all one wants, is *exclusively* the Divine.

"I want nothing but the Divine, I think of nothing but the Divine, I do nothing but what will lead me to the Divine, I love nothing but the Divine."

Try – try, just to see, try for half an hour, you will see how difficult it is! And during that time take great care that there isn't a part of the vital or a part of the mind or a part of the physical being nicely hidden there, at the back, so that you don't see it (*Mother hides her hands behind her back*) and don't notice that it is not collaborating – sitting quietly there so that you don't unearth it... it says nothing, but it does not change, it hides itself. How many such parts! How many parts hide themselves! You put them in your pocket because you don't want to see them or else they get behind your back and sit there well-hidden, right in the middle of your back, so as not to be seen. When you go there with your torch – your torch of sincerity – you ferret out all the corners, everywhere, all the small corners which do not consent, the things which say "No" or those which do not move: "I am not going to budge. I am glued to this place of mine and nothing will make me move."... You have a torch there with you, and you flash it upon the thing, upon everything. You will see there are many of them there, behind your back, well stuck.[160]

THE MOTHER

The one condition of getting rid of things [inner obstacles] is an absolute central sincerity in all the parts of the being, and that means an absolute insistence on the Truth and nothing but the Truth. There will then be a readiness for unsparing self-criticism and vigilant openness to the light, an uneasiness when falsehood comes in, which will finally purify the whole being.

The defects mentioned are more or less common in various degrees in almost every sadhak, though there are some who are not touched by them. They can be got rid of, if the requisite sincerity is there. But if they occupy the central parts of the being and vitiate the attitude, then the sadhak will give a constant open or covert support to them, his mind will always be ready to give disguises and justifications and try to elude the searchlight of the self-critical faculty and protests of the psychic being. That means a failure in the yoga at least for this existence.[161]

SRI AUROBINDO

How are we to know, you will ask, when it is the Divine Will that makes us act? The Divine Will is not difficult to recognise. It is unmistakable. You can know it without being very far on the path. Only you must listen to its voice, the small voice that is here in the heart. Once you are accustomed to listen, if you do anything that is contrary to the Divine Will, you feel an uneasiness. If you persist on the wrong track, you get very much disturbed. If, however, you give some material excuse as the cause of your uneasiness and proceed on your way, you gradually lose the faculty of perception and finally you may go on doing all kinds of wrong and feel no uneasiness. But if, when once you feel the least disturbance, you stop and ask of your inner self, "What is the cause of this?" then you do get the real answer and the whole thing becomes quite clear. Do not try to give a material excuse when you feel a little depression or a slight uneasiness. When you stop and look about for the reason, be absolutely straight and sincere. At first your mind will construct a very plausible and beautiful explanation. Do not accept it, but look beyond and ask, "What is it that is behind this movement? Why am I doing this?" Finally you will discover, hidden in a corner, the little ripple – a slight wrong turn or twist in your attitude that is causing the trouble or disturbance.[162]

THE MOTHER

*Those who take error for truth, and the truth for error, will never attain the supreme goal, for they are led astray by vain desires and false views.*

The Dhammapada

... My experience is like this: whenever you sincerely want to know the truth, you do know it. There is *always* something to point out the error to you, to make you recognise the truth. And if you observe yourself attentively you find out that it is because you prefer error that you do not find the truth.

Even in small details, the very smallest – not to speak of the big things of life, the big decisions that one has to take – even in the smallest things, whenever the aspiration for the truth and the will to be true are wholly sincere, the indication always comes. And precisely, with the method of the Buddhist discipline, if you follow up within yourself the causes of your way of being, you always find out that persistence in error comes from desire. It is because you have the preference, the desire to feel, to act, to think in a particular way, that you make the mistake. It is not simply because you do not know what is true. You do not know it precisely because you say in a vague, general, imprecise way, "Oh, I want the truth." In fact, if you take a detail, each detail, and put your finger on it, you discover that you are playing the ostrich in order not to see. You put up something uncertain, something vague, a veil, in order not to see behind it.

Whenever there is sincerity, you find that the help, the guidance, the grace are always there to give you the answer and you are not mistaken for long.

It is this sincerity in the aspiration for progress, in the will for truth, in the need to be truly pure – pure as it is understood in the spiritual life – it is this sincerity which is the key to all progress. With it you know – and you *can*.

There is always, somewhere in the being, something which prefers to deceive itself, otherwise the light is there, always ready to guide, but you shut your eyes in order not to see it.[163]

THE MOTHER

### 3. Personal Effort and Surrender

There are two possibilities, one of purification by personal effort, which takes a long time, another by a direct intervention of the Divine Grace which is usually rapid in its action. For the latter there must be a complete surrender and self-giving and for that again usually it is necessary to have a mind that can remain quite quiet and allow the Divine Force to act supporting it with its complete adhesion at every step, but otherwise remaining still and quiet. This last condition which resembles the baby-cat attitude spoken of by Ramakrishna, is difficult to have. Those who are accustomed to a very active movement of their thought and will in all they do, find it difficult to still the activity and adopt the quietude of mental self-giving. This does not mean that they cannot do the yoga or cannot arrive at self-giving – only the purification and the self-giving take a long time to accomplish and one must have the patience and steady perseverance and resolution to go through.[164]

SRI AUROBINDO

A complete surrender is not possible in so short a time, – for a complete surrender means to cut the knot of the ego in each part of the being and offer it, free and whole, to the Divine. The mind, the vital, the physical consciousness (and even each part of these in all its movements) have one after the other to surrender separately, to give up their own way and to accept the way of the Divine. But what one can do is to make from the beginning a central resolve and self-dedication and to implement it in whatever way one finds open, at each step, taking advantage of each occasion that offers itself to make the self-giving complete. A surrender in one direction makes others easier, more inevitable; but it does not of itself cut or loosen the other knots, and especially those which are very intimately bound up with the present personality and its most cherished formations may often present great difficulties, even after the central will has been fixed and the first seals put on its resolve in practice.[165]

SRI AUROBINDO

It [the attitude of surrender] cannot be absolutely complete in the beginning, but it can be true – if the central will is sincere and there is the faith and the Bhakti. There may be contrary movements, but these will be unable to stand for long and the imperfection of the surrender in the lower part will not seriously interfere.[166]

SRI AUROBINDO

There is nothing unintelligible in what I say about strength and Grace. Strength has a value for spiritual realisation, but to say that it can be done by strength only and by no other means is a violent exaggeration. Grace is not an invention, it is a fact of spiritual experience. Many who would be considered as mere nothings by the wise and strong have attained by Grace; illiterate, without mental power or training, without "strength" of character or will, they have yet aspired and suddenly or rapidly grown into spiritual realisation, because they had faith or because they were sincere... these facts... are facts of spiritual history and of quite ordinary spiritual experience....

Strength, if it is spiritual, is a power for spiritual realisation; a greater power is sincerity; the greatest power of all is Grace. I have said times without number that if a man is sincere, he will go through in spite of long delay and overwhelming difficulties. I have repeatedly spoken of the Divine Grace. I have referred any number of times to the line of the Gita:

"I will deliver thee from all sin and evil, do not grieve."[167]

SRI AUROBINDO

It [the idea that the sadhana is done by the Divine rather than by oneself] is a truth but a truth that does not become effective for the consciousness until or in proportion as it is realised. The people who stagnate because of it are those who accept the idea but do not realise – so they have neither the force of tapasya nor that of the Divine Grace. On the other hand those who can realise it feel even behind their tapasya and in it the action of the Divine Force.[168]

SRI AUROBINDO

Talk of surrender or a mere idea or tepid wish for integral consecration will not do; there must be the push for a radical and total change.

It is not by taking a mere mental attitude that this can be done or even by any number of inner experiences which leave the outer man as he was. It is this outer man who has to open, to surrender and to change. His every least movement, habit, action has to be surrendered, seen, held up and exposed to the divine Light, offered to the divine Force for its old forms and motives to be destroyed and the divine Truth and the action of the transforming consciousness of the Divine Mother to take their place.[169]

SRI AUROBINDO

If there is not a complete surrender, then it is not possible to adopt the baby-cat attitude, – it becomes mere tamasic passivity calling itself surrender. If a complete surrender is not possible in the beginning, it follows that personal effort is necessary.[170]

SRI AUROBINDO

### 4. Confidence, Faith and Trust

*Just as the strong wind has no hold upon a mighty rock, so Mara has no hold upon a man who does not live in pursuit of pleasure, who has good control of his senses, who knows how to moderate his appetite, who is endowed with unshakable faith and who wastes not his energies.*

The Dhammapada

What the Dhammapada means when it speaks of faith is

not at all the belief in a dogma or a religion, it is not even faith in the teaching of the Master; it is faith in one's own possibilities, the certitude that whatever the difficulties, whatever the obstacles, whatever the imperfections, even the negations in the being, one is born for the realisation and one *will* realise.

The will must never falter, the effort must be persevering and the faith unshakable. Then instead of spending years to realise what one has to realise, one can do it in a few months, sometimes even in a few days and, if there is sufficient intensity, in a few hours. That is to say, you can take a position within yourself and no bad will that attacks the realisation will have any more power over you than the storm has over a rock.

After that, the way is no longer difficult; it becomes extraordinarily interesting.[171]

THE MOTHER

The best way of meeting difficulties is a quiet and calm confidence in the Grace.[172]

THE MOTHER

Keep faith and confidence and remain cheerful.[173]

THE MOTHER

Be confident, you will become what you have to be and achieve what you have to do.[174]

THE MOTHER

One must have entire confidence in the Victory of the Divine – and this general Victory will include in itself the personal victory of all who will have remained faithful and confident.[175]

THE MOTHER

With confidence we shall advance; with certitude we shall wait.[176]

THE MOTHER

Faith is the soul's witness to something not yet manifested, achieved or realised, but which yet the Knower within us, even in the absence of all indications, feels to be true or supremely worth following or achieving. This thing within us can last even when there is no fixed belief in the mind, even when the vital struggles and revolts and refuses. Who is there that practises the yoga and has not his periods, long periods of disappointment and failure and disbelief and darkness? But there is something that sustains him and even goes on in spite of himself, because it feels that what it followed after was yet true and it more than feels, it knows. The fundamental faith in yoga is this, inherent in the soul, that the Divine exists and the Divine is the one thing to be followed after – nothing else in life is worth having in comparison with that. So long as a man has that faith, he is marked for the spiritual life and I will say that, even if his nature is full of obstacles and crammed with denials and difficulties, and even if he has many years of struggle, he is marked out for success in the spiritual life.

It is this faith that you need to develop – a faith which is in accordance with reason and common sense – that if the Divine exists and has called you to the Path, (as is evident), then there must be a Divine Guidance behind and through and in spite of all difficulties you will arrive. Not to listen to the hostile voices that suggest failure or to the voices of impatient, vital haste that echo them, not to believe that because great difficulties are there, there can be no success or that because the Divine has not yet shown himself he will never show himself, but to take the position that everyone takes when he fixes his mind on a great and difficult goal, "I will go on till I succeed – all difficulties notwithstanding". To which the believer in the Divine adds, "The Divine exists, my following after the Divine cannot fail. I will go on through everything till I find him".[177]

SRI AUROBINDO

Even a faltering faith and a slow and partial surrender have their force and their result, otherwise only the rare few could do sadhana at all. What I mean by the central faith is a faith in the soul or the central being behind, a faith which is there even when the mind doubts and the vital despairs and the physical wants to collapse, and after the attack is over reappears and pushes on the path again. It may be strong and bright, it may be pale and in appearance weak, but if it persists each time in going on, it is the real thing.[178]

SRI AUROBINDO

The way to get faith and all things else is to insist on having them and refuse to flag or despair or give up until one has them – it is the way by which everything has been got since this difficult earth began to have thinking and aspiring creatures upon it. It is to open always, always to the Light and turn one's back on the Darkness. It is to refuse the voices that say persistently, "You cannot, you shall not, you are incapable, you are the puppet of a dream," – for these are the enemy voices, they cut one off from the result that was coming, by their strident clamour and then triumphantly point to the barrenness of the result as a proof of their thesis. The difficulty of the endeavour is a known thing, but the difficult is not the impossible – it is the difficult that has always been accomplished and the conquest of difficulties makes up all that is valuable in the earth's history. In the spiritual endeavour also it shall be so.

You have only to set about resolutely slaying the Rakshasa and the doors will open to you as they have done to many others who were held up by their own mind or vital nature.[179]

SRI AUROBINDO

We have to have the faith that in spite of our ignorance and errors and weaknesses and in spite of the attacks of hostile forces and in spite of any immediate appearance of failure the Divine Will is leading us, through every circumstance, towards the final Realisation. This faith will give us equanimity; it is a faith that accepts what happens, not definitively but as something that has to be gone through on the way.[180]

SRI AUROBINDO

Faith, reliance upon God, surrender and self-giving to the Divine Power are necessary and indispensable. But reliance upon God must not be made an excuse for indolence, weakness and surrender to the impulses of the lower Nature: it must go along with untiring aspiration and a persistent rejection of all that comes in the way of the Divine Truth. The surrender to the Divine must not be turned into an excuse, a cloak or an occasion for surrender to one's own desires and lower movements or to one's ego...[181]

SRI AUROBINDO

Faith and courage are the true attitude to keep in life and work always and in the spiritual experience also.[182]

SRI AUROBINDO

In moments of trial faith in the divine protection and the call for that protection; at all times the faith that what the Divine wills is the best.[183]

SRI AUROBINDO

If you desire only the Divine, there is an absolute certitude that you will reach the Divine, but all these questionings and repinings at each movement only delay and keep an impending curtain before the heart and the eyes. For at every step, when one makes an advance, the opposite forces will throw these doubts like a rope between the legs and stop one short with a stumble – it is their *métier* to do that.... One must say, "Since I want only the Divine, my success is sure, I have only to walk forward in all confidence and His own Hand will be there secretly leading me to Him by His own way and at His own time." That is what you must keep as your constant mantra. Anything else one may doubt but that he who desires only the Divine shall reach the Divine is a certitude and more certain than two and two make four. That is the faith every sadhak must have at the bottom of his heart, supporting him through every stumble and blow and ordeal.[184]

SRI AUROBINDO

Keep firm faith in the victory of the Light and face with calm equanimity the resistances of Matter and human personality to their own transformation.[185]

SRI AUROBINDO

It is not a hope but a certitude that the complete transformation of the nature will take place.[186]

SRI AUROBINDO

Even if there is much darkness – and this world is full of it and the physical nature of man also – yet a ray of the true Light can prevail eventually against a tenfold darkness. Believe that and cleave to it always.[187]

SRI AUROBINDO

The core of the inner surrender is trust and confidence in the Divine. One takes the attitude: "I want the Divine and nothing else. I want to give myself entirely to him and since my soul wants that, it cannot be but that I shall meet and realise him. I ask nothing but that and his action in me to bring me to him, his action secret or open, veiled or manifest. I do not insist on my own time and way; let him do all in his own time and way; I shall believe in him, accept his will, aspire steadily for his light and presence and joy, go through all difficulties and delays, relying on him and never giving up. Let my mind be quiet and trust him and let him open it to his light; let my vital be quiet and turn to him alone and let him open it to his calm and joy. All for him and myself for him. Whatever happens, I will keep to this aspiration and self-giving and go on in perfect reliance that it will be done."

That is the attitude into which one must grow; for certainly it cannot be made perfect at once – mental and vital movements come across – but if one keeps the will to it, it will grow in the being.[188]

SRI AUROBINDO

For those who have within them a sincere call for the Divine, however the mind or vital may present difficulties or attacks come or the progress be slow and painful, – even if they fall back or fall away from the path for a time, the psychic always prevails in the end and the Divine Help proves effective. Trust in that and persevere – then the goal is sure.[189]

SRI AUROBINDO

*... what is the difference between faith and trust?*

Faith is something... much more integral than trust. You see, you have trust in the Divine, in the sense that you are convinced that all that comes from Him will always be the best for you: whatever His decision and whatever the experience He sends you or the circumstances in which He puts you, it will all be always what is best for you. This is trust. But faith – that kind of unshakable certitude in the very existence of God – faith is something that seizes the whole being. It is not only mental, psychic or vital: it is the whole being, entirely, which has faith. Faith leads straight to experience.

### Can't trust be total and entire?

Not necessarily. Well, there is a shade of difference – however, I don't know, it is not the same thing.

One has given oneself totally to the divine work, one has faith in it, not only in its possibility, but faith that it is *the* thing which is true and which must be, and one gives oneself entirely to it, without asking what will happen. And so, therein or thereon may be grafted a certitude, a confidence that one is capable of accomplishing it, that is, of participating in it and doing it because one has given oneself to it – a confidence that what one is going to do, what one wants to do, one will be able to do; that this realisation one wants to attain, one will attain. The first does not put any questions, does not think of the results: it gives itself entirely – it gives itself and then that's all. It is something that absorbs one completely. The other may be grafted upon it. Confidence says: "Yes, I shall participate, realise what I want to realise, I shall surely take part in this work." For the other, one has faith in the Divine, that it is the Divine who is all, and can do all, and does all... and who is the only real existence – and one gives oneself entirely to this faith, to the Divine, that's all. One has faith in the existence of the Divine and gives oneself; and there can also be grafted upon this a trust that this relation one has with the Divine, this faith one has in the Divine, will work in such a way that all that happens to him – whatever it may be, all that happens to him – will not only be an expression of the divine will (that of course is understood) but also the best that could happen, that nothing better could have happened to him, since it is the Divine who is doing it for him. This attitude is not necessarily a part of faith, for faith does not question anything, it does not ask what the consequence of its self-giving will be – it gives itself, and – that's all; while confidence can come and say, "That's what the result will be." And this is an absolute fact, that is, the moment one gives oneself entirely to the Divine, without calculating, in a total faith, without bargaining of any kind – one gives oneself, and then, come what may! "That does not concern me, I just give myself" – automatically it will always be for you, in all circumstances, at every moment, the best that will happen... not the way you conceive of it (naturally, thought knows nothing), but in reality. Well, there is a part of the being which can become aware of this and have this confidence. This is something added on to faith which gives it more strength, a strength – how shall I put it? – of total acceptance and the best utilisation of what happens.[190]

THE MOTHER

### 5. Patience, Perseverance, Endurance, Cheerfulness

It is certain that an ardent aspiration helps to progress, but patience is also needed. For it is a very big change that has to be made and, although there can be moments of great rapidity, it is never all the time like that. Old things try to stick as much as possible; the new that come have to develop and the consciousness takes time to assimilate them and make them normal to the nature.[191]

SRI AUROBINDO

You must arm yourself with an endless patience and endurance. You do a thing once, ten times, a hundred times, a thousand times if necessary, but you do it till it gets done. And not done only here and there, but everywhere and everywhere at the same time. This is the great problem one sets oneself. That is why, to those who come to tell me very light-heartedly, "I want to do yoga", I reply, "Think it over, one may do the yoga for a number of years without noticing the least result. But if you want to do it, you must perist and persist with such a will that you should be ready to do it for ten lifetimes, a hundred lifetimes if necessary, in order to succeed." I do not say it will be like that, but the *attitude* must be like that.[192]

THE MOTHER

No sadhak even if he had the capacity of the ancient Rishis and Tapaswis or the strength of a Vivekananda can hope to keep during the early years of his sadhana a continuous good condition or union with the Divine or an unbroken call or height of aspiration. It takes a long time to spiritualise the whole nature and until that is done, variations must come. A constant trust and patience must be cultivated – must be acquired – not least when things go against – for when they are favourable, trust and patience are easy.[193]

SRI AUROBINDO

The power needed in yoga is the power to go through effort, difficulty or trouble without getting fatigued, depressed, discouraged or impatient and without breaking off the effort or giving up one's aim or resolution.[194]

SRI AUROBINDO

Whatever method is used, persistence and perseverance are essential. For whatever method is used, the complexity of the natural resistance will be there to combat it.[195]

SRI AUROBINDO

The difficulties have to be faced and the more cheerfully they are faced, the sooner they will be overcome. The one thing to do is to keep the mantra of success, the determination of victory, the fixed resolve, "Have it I must and have it I will." Impossible? There is no such thing as impossibility – there are difficulties and things of *longue haleine*, but no impossibles. What one is determined fixedly to do will get done now or later – it becomes possible. Drive out dark despair and go bravely on with your yoga. As the darkness disappears, the inner doors will open.[196]

SRI AUROBINDO

Whether by tapasya or surrender does not matter, the one thing is to be firm in setting one's face to the goal. Once one has set one's feet on the way, how can one draw back from it to something inferior? If one keeps firm, falls do not matter, one rises up again and goes forward. If one is firm towards the goal, there can be on the way to the Divine no eventual failure. And if there is something within you that drives as surely there is, falterings or falls or failure of faith make no eventual difference. One has to go on till the struggle is over and there is the straight and open and thornless way before us.[197]

SRI AUROBINDO

You have only to remain quiet and firm in your following of the path and your will to go to the end. If you do that circumstances will in the end be obliged to shape themselves to your will, because it will be the Divine Will in you.[198]

SRI AUROBINDO

... if you are not able to face difficulties without getting discouraged and without giving up, because it is too difficult; and if you are incapable... well, of receiving blows and yet continuing, of "pocketing" them, as they say – when you receive blows as a result of your defects, of putting them in your pocket and continuing to go forward without flagging – you don't go very far; at the first turning where you lose sight of your little habitual life, you fall into despair and give up the game.

The most... how shall I put it? the most material form of

this [quality of endurance] is perseverance. Unless you are resolved to begin the same thing over again a thousand times if need be... You know, people come to me in despair, "But I thought it was done and now I must begin again!" And if they are told, "But that's nothing, you will probably have to begin again a hundred times, two hundred times, a thousand times; you take one step forward and think you are secure, but there will always be something to bring back the same difficulty a little farther on. You think you have solved the problem, you must solve it yet once again; it will turn up again looking just a little different, but it will be the same problem", and if you are not determined that: "Even if it comes back a million times, I shall do it a million times, but I shall go through with it", well, you won't be able to do the yoga. This is absolutely indispensable.

People have a beautiful experience and say, "Ah, now this is it!..." And then it settles down, diminishes, gets veiled, and suddenly something quite unexpected, absolutely commonplace and apparently completely uninteresting comes before you and blocks your way. And then you say, "Ah! what's the good of having made this progress if it's going to start all over again? Why should I do it? I made an effort, I succeeded, achieved something, and now it's as if I had done nothing! It's indeed hopeless." For you have no endurance.

If one has endurance, one says, "It's all right. Good, I shall begin again as often as necessary; a thousand times, ten thousand times, a hundred thousand times if necessary, I shall begin again – but I shall go to the end and nothing will have the power to stop me on the way."[199]

THE MOTHER

Let endurance be your watchword: teach the lifeforce in you – your vital being – not to complain but to put up with all the conditions necessary for great achievement. The body is a very enduring servant, it bears the stress of circumstance tamely like a beast of burden. It is the vital being that is always grumbling and uneasy. The slavery and torture to which it subjects the physical is almost incalculable. How it twists and deforms the poor body to its own fads and fancies, irrationally demanding that everything should be shaped according to its whimsicality! But the very essence of endurance is that the vital should learn to give up its capricious likes and dislikes and preserve an equanimity in the midst of the most trying conditions. When you are treated roughly by somebody or you lack something which would relieve your discomfort, you must keep up cheerfully instead of letting yourself be disturbed. Let nothing ruffle you the least bit, and whenever the vital tends to air its petty grievances with pompous exaggeration just stop to consider how very happy you are, compared to so many in this world.[200]

THE MOTHER

There is nothing spiritually wrong in being glad and cheerful, on the contrary it is the right thing. As for struggles and aspiration, struggles are really not indispensable to progress and there are many people who get so habituated to the struggling attitude that they have all the time struggles and very little else. That is not desirable. There is a sunlit path as well as a gloomy one and it is the better of the two.[201]

SRI AUROBINDO

Certainly if one is satisfied with life, entranced by it so that it shuts out the sense of the soul within or hampers the attraction to the Divine, then a period of *vairāgya,* sorrow, depression, a painful breaking of the vital ties may be necessary and many go through that. But once the turn made, it should be to the one direction and a perpetual *vairāgya* is not needed. Nor when we speak of cheerfulness as the best condition, do we mean a cheerful following of the vital life, but a cheerful following of the path to the Divine which is not impossible if the mind and heart take the right view and posture. At any rate, if positive cheerfulness is not possible in one's case, still one should not acquiesce in or mentally support a constant depression and sadness.[202]

SRI AUROBINDO

Cheerfulness is the salt of sadhana. It is a thousand times better than gloominess.[203]

SRI AUROBINDO

It [cheerfulness] puts you in the right condition for the psychic to work and without knowing it you grow in just the right perceptions and right feelings for the spiritual attitude.[204]

SRI AUROBINDO

All depression and gloom is created by the hostile forces who are never so pleased as when throwing on you a melancholy mood.... Therefore, face your troubles joyously, oppose with invariable cheerfulness the obstacles that beset the road to transformation. The best means of routing the enemy is to laugh in his face! You may grapple and tussle for days and he may still show an undiminished vigour; but just once laugh at him and lo! he takes to his heels. A laugh of self-confidence and of faith in the Divine is the most shattering strength possible – it disrupts the enemy's front, spreads havoc in his ranks and carries you triumphantly onwards.

The converted vital feels... a joy in the process of realisation. All the difficulties implied in that process it accepts with gusto, it never feels happier than when the Truth is shown it and the play of falsehood in its lower nature laid bare. It does not do the Yoga as if carrying a burden on its back but as if it were a very pleasurable occupation. It is willing to endure the utmost with a smile if it is a condition of the transformation. Neither complaining nor grumbling, it endures happily because it is for the sake of the Divine that it does so. It has the unshakable conviction that the victory will be won.[205]

THE MOTHER

... the more you advance, the more vigilant must you become. And the most essential quality is perseverance, endurance, and a... what shall I call it? – a kind of inner good humour which helps you not to get discouraged, not to become sad, and to face all difficulties with a smile. There is an English word which expresses this very well – cheerfulness. If you can keep this within you, you fight much better, resist much better, in the light, these bad influences which try to hinder you from progressing.[206]

THE MOTHER

A smile acts upon difficulties as the sun upon clouds – it disperses them.[207]

THE MOTHER

Someone who knows how to smile in all circumstances is very close to true equality of soul.[208]

THE MOTHER

Generally speaking, man is an animal who takes himself terribly seriously. To know how to smile at oneself in all circumstances, to smile at one's sorrows and disillusions, ambitions and sufferings, indignation and revolt – what a powerful weapon with which to overcome oneself![209]

THE MOTHER

Learn to smile always and in all circumstances; to smile at your sorrows as well as your joys, your sufferings as well as your hopes, for in a smile there is a sovereign power of self-mastery.[210]

THE MOTHER

## 6. Awareness and Vigilance

To be conscious, first of all. We are conscious of only an insignificant portion of our being; for the most part we are unconscious. It is this unconsciousness that keeps us down to our unregenerate nature and prevents change and transformation in it. It is through unconsciousness that the undivine forces enter into us and make us their slaves.

You are to be conscious of yourself, you must awake to your nature and movements, you must know why and how you do things or feel or think them; you must understand your motives and impulses, the forces, hidden and apparent, that move you; in fact, you must, as it were, take to pieces the entire machinery of your being. Once you are conscious, it means that you can distinguish and sift things, you can see which are the forces that pull you down and which help you on. And when you know the right from the wrong, the true from the false, the divine from the undivine, you are to act strictly up to your knowledge; that is to say, resolutely reject one and accept the other. The duality will present itself at every step and at every step you will have to make your choice. You will have to be patient and persistent and vigilant – "sleepless", as the adepts say...[211]

THE MOTHER

*Is it the same thing... to be conscious... and to master the different parts of the being?*

One precedes the other. First of all one must be conscious, then control, and by continuing the mastery one changes one's character. Changing the character is what comes last. One must control bad habits, the old habits, for a very long time for them to drop off and the character to change.

We may take the example of someone who has frequent depressions. When things are not exactly as he would like them to be, he becomes depressed. So, to begin with, he must become aware of his depression – not only of the depression but of the causes of depression, why he gets depressed so easily. Then, once he has become conscious, he must master the depressions, must stop being depressed even when the cause of depression is there – he must master his depression, stop it from coming. And finally, after this work has been done for a sufficiently long time, the nature loses the habit of having depressions and no longer reacts in the same way, the nature is changed.[212]

THE MOTHER

*Vigilance is the way that leads to immortality (or Nirvana). Negligence is the way that leads to death. Those who are vigilant do not die. Those who are negligent are dead already.*

The Dhammapada

... Vigilance means to be awake, to be on one's guard, to be sincere – never to be taken by surprise. When you want to do sadhana, at each moment of your life, there is a choice between taking a step that leads to the goal and falling asleep or sometimes even going backwards, telling yourself, "Oh, later on, not immediately" – sitting down on the way.

To be vigilant is not merely to resist what pulls you downward, but above all to be alert in order not to lose any opportunity to progress, any opportunity to overcome a weakness, to resist a temptation, any opportunity to learn something, to correct something, to master something. If you are vigilant, you can do in a few days what would otherwise take years. If you are vigilant, you change each circumstance of your life, each action, each movement into an occasion for coming nearer the goal.

There are two kinds of vigilance, active and passive. There is a vigilance that gives you a warning if you are about to make a mistake, if you are making a wrong choice, if you are being weak or allowing yourself to be tempted, and there is the active vigilance which seeks an opportunity to progress, seeks to utilise every circumstance to advance more quickly.

There is a difference between preventing yourself from falling and advancing more quickly.

And both are absolutely necessary.

He who is not vigilant is already dead. He has lost contact with the true purpose of existence and of life.

So the hours, circumstances, life pass in vain, bringing nothing, and you awake from your somnolence in a hole from which it is very difficult to escape.[213]

THE MOTHER

... only you must remain vigilant always. For when the condition is good, the lower movements have a habit of subsiding and become quiescent, hiding as it were, – or they go out of the nature and remain at a distance. But if they see that the sadhak is losing vigilance, then they slowly begin to rise or draw near, most often unseen, and when he is quite off his guard, surge up suddenly or make a sudden irruption. This continues until the whole nature, mental, vital, physical down to the very subconscient is enlightened, conscious, full of the Divine. Till that happens, one must always remain watchful in a sleepless vigilance.[214]

SRI AUROBINDO

It is perhaps that the attitude you took of going on with the calm within and slowly changing what had to be changed, postponing certain things for the future, – though not a wrong attitude in itself, made you somewhat lax, allowing things to play on the surface (desires, etc.) which should have been kept in check. This resolution may have opened the way for the old movements to rise through this part which was not yet ready to change at all and the hostile forces finding you off your guard took the opportunity to push the attack home. They are always vigilant for an opportunity and there must be a sufficient vigilance on the sadhak's side to refuse it to them.[215]

SRI AUROBINDO

### 7. The Witness Attitude – Detachment

There is a stage in the sadhana in which the inner being begins to awake. Often the first result is the condition made up of the following elements:

1. A sort of witness attitude in which the inner consciousness looks at all that happens as a spectator or observer, observing things but taking no active interest or pleasure in them.

2. A state of neutral equanimity in which there is neither joy nor sorrow, only quietude.

3. A sense of being something separate from all that happens, observing it but not part of it.[216]

SRI AUROBINDO

The consciousness you speak of would be described in the

Gita as the witness Purusha. The Purusha or basic consciousness is the true being or at least, in whatever plane it
manifests, represents the true being. But in the ordinary
nature of man it is covered up by the ego and the ignorant
play of the Prakriti and remains veiled behind as the
unseen Witness supporting the play of the Ignorance.
When it emerges, you feel it as a consciousness behind,
calm, central, unidentified with the play which depends
upon it. It may be covered over, but it is always there. The
emergence of the Purusha is the beginning of liberation.
But it can also become slowly the Master – slowly because
the whole habit of the ego and the play of the lower forces
is against that. Still it can dictate what higher play is to
replace the lower movement and then there is the process
of that replacement, the higher coming, the lower struggling to remain and push away the higher movement.[217]

SRI AUROBINDO

By itself the Purusha is impersonal, but by mixing itself
with the movements of Prakriti it makes for itself a surface
of ego and personality. When it appears in its own
separate nature then it is seen to be detached and
observing.[218]

SRI AUROBINDO

The attitude of the witness consciousness within – I do not
think it necessarily involves an external seclusion, though
one may do that also – is a very necessary stage in the
progress. It helps the liberation from the lower Prakriti
– not getting involved in the ordinary nature movements;

it helps the establishment of a perfect calm and peace within, for there is then one part of the being which remains detached and sees without being disturbed the perturbations of the surface; it helps also the ascent into the higher consciousness and the descent of the higher consciousness, for it is through this calm, detached and liberated inner being that the ascent and descent can easily be done. Also, to have the same witness look on the movements of Prakriti in others, seeing, understanding but not perturbed by them in any way is a very great help towards both the liberation and the universalisation of the being....

As for the surrender it is not inconsistent with the witness attitude. On the contrary by liberating from the ordinary Prakriti, it makes easier the surrender to the higher or divine Power. Very often when this witness attitude has not been taken but there is a successful calling in of the Force to act in one, one of the first things the Force does is to establish the witness attitude so as to be able to act with less interference or immixture from the movements of the lower Prakriti.[219]

SRI AUROBINDO

To be perfectly sincere it is indispensable not to have any preference, any desire, any attraction, any dislike, any sympathy or antipathy, any attachment, any repulsion. One must have a total, integral vision of things, in which everything is in its place and one has the same attitude towards all things: the attitude of true vision. This programme is obviously very difficult for a human being to realise. Unless he has decided to divinise himself, it

seems almost impossible that he could be free from all
these contraries within him. And yet, so long as one
carries them in himself, one cannot be perfectly sincere.
Automatically the mental, the vital and even the physical
working is falsified. I am emphasising the physical, for
even the working of the senses is warped: one does not
see, hear, taste, feel things as they are in reality as long as
one has a preference. So long as there are things which
please you and others which don't, so long as you are
attracted by certain things, and repulsed by others, you
cannot see things in their reality; you see them through
your reaction, your preference or your repulsion. The
senses are instruments which get out of order, in the same
way as sensations, feelings and thoughts. Therefore, to be
sure of what you see, what you feel, what you experience
and think, you must have a complete detachment; and this
is obviously not an easy task. But until then your perception cannot be wholly true, and so it is not sincere.[220]

THE MOTHER

You can certainly go on developing the consciousness of
the Witness Purusha above, but if it is only a witness and
the lower Prakriti is allowed to have its own way, there
would be no reason why these conditions should ever
stop. Many take that attitude – that the Purusha has to
liberate itself by standing apart, and the Prakriti can be
allowed to go on till the end of the life doing its own
business – it is *prārabdha karma*; when the body falls
away, the Prakriti will drop also and the Purusha go off
into the featureless Brahman! This is a comfortable
theory, but of more than doubtful truth; I don't think

liberation is so simple and facile a matter as that. In any case, the transformation which is the object of our yoga would not take place.

The Purusha above is not only a Witness, he is the giver (or withholder) of the sanction; if he persistently refuses the sanction to a movement of Prakriti, keeping himself detached, then, even if it goes on for a time by its past momentum, it usually loses its hold after a time, becomes more feeble, less persistent, less concrete and in the end fades away. If you take the Purusha consciousness, it should be not only as the Witness but as the Anumanta, refusing sanction to the disturbing movements, sanctioning only peace, calm, purity and whatever else is part of the divine nature. This refusal of sanction need not mean a struggle with the lower Prakriti; it should be a quiet, persistent, detached refusal leaving unsupported, unassented to, without meaning or justification, the contrary action of the nature.[221]

SRI AUROBINDO

Detachment is the beginning of mastery, but for complete mastery there should be no reactions at all. When there is something within undisturbed by the reactions that means the inner being is free and master of itself, but it is not yet master of the whole nature. When it is master, it allows no wrong reactions – if any come they are at once repelled and shaken off, and finally none come at all.[222]

SRI AUROBINDO

## 8. Rejection

Divinisation itself does not mean the destruction of the human elements; it means taking them up, showing them the way to their own perfection, raising them by purification and perfection to their full power and Ananda and that means the raising of the whole of earthly life to its full power and Ananda.[223]

SRI AUROBINDO

Unfortunately, there *is* the resistance, a very obscure and obstinate resistance. That necessitates a negative element in the yoga, an element of rejection of things that stand in the way and of pressure upon those forms that are crude and useless to disappear, on those that are useful but imperfect or have been perverted to retain or to recover their true movement. To the vital this pressure is painful, first, because it is obscure and does not understand and, secondly, because there are parts of it that want to be left to their crude motions and not to change. That is why the intervention of a psychic attitude is so helpful. For the psychic has the happy confidence, the ready understanding and response, the spontaneous surrender....[224]

SRI AUROBINDO

The rejection of desire is essentially the rejection of the element of craving, putting that out from the consciousness itself as a foreign element not belonging to the true self and the inner nature. But refusal to indulge the suggestions of desire is also a part of the rejection; to abstain from the action suggested, if it is not the right action, must be included in the yogic discipline. It is only when this is done in the wrong way, by a mental ascetic principle or a hard moral rule, that it can be called suppression. The difference between suppression and an inward essential rejection is the difference between mental or moral control and a spiritual purification.

When one lives in the true consciousness one feels the desires outside oneself, entering from outside, from the universal lower Prakriti, into the mind and the vital parts. In the ordinary human condition this is not felt; men become aware of the desire only when it is there, when it has come inside and found a lodging or a habitual harbourage and so they think it is their own and a part of themselves. The first condition for getting rid of desire is, therefore, to become conscious with the true consciousness; for then it becomes much easier to dismiss it than when one has to struggle with it as if it were a constituent part of oneself to be thrown out from the being. It is easier to cast off an accretion than to excise what is felt as a parcel of our substance.

When the psychic being is in front, then also to get rid of desire becomes easy; for the psychic being has in itself no desires, it has only aspirations and a seeking and love for the Divine and all things that are or tend towards the Divine. The constant prominence of the psychic being tends of itself to bring out the true consciousness and set right almost automatically the movements of the nature.[225]

SRI AUROBINDO

It is true that the mere suppression or holding down of

desire is not enough, not by itself truly effective, but that
does not mean that desires are to be indulged; it means
that desires have not merely to be suppressed, but to be
rejected from the nature. In place of desire there must be
a single-minded aspiration towards the Divine.[226]

SRI AUROBINDO

Your theory is a mistaken one. The free expression of a
passion may relieve the vital for a time, but at the same
time it gives it a right to return always. It is not reduced at
all. Suppression with inner indulgence in subtle forms is
not a cure, but expression in outer indulgence is still less a
cure. It is perfectly possible to go on without manifestation if one is resolute to arrive at a complete control, the
control being not a mere suppression but an inner and
outer rejection.[227]

SRI AUROBINDO

Vital desire grows by being indulged, it does not become
satisfied. If your desire were indulged, it would begin to
grow more and more and ask for more and more. That has
been our constant experience with the sadhaks and it
confirms what has always been known about desire.
Desire and envy have to be thrown out of the consciousness – there is no other way to deal with them.[228]

SRI AUROBINDO

Not necessarily suppression, if the refusal of food [to a
desire] is accompanied by detachment in the major part of

the being. The difference between suppression (*nigraha*)
and self-control (*saṁyama*) is that one says "I cannot help
desiring but I will not satisfy my desire", while the other
says "I refuse the desire as well as the satisfaction of the
desire".[229]

SRI AUROBINDO

*Nigraha* means holding down the movement, but a
movement merely held down is only suspended – it is
better to reject and dismiss, detaching yourself from it.[230]

SRI AUROBINDO

Everything which it hankers after is desirable to the
vital – but the desire has to be rejected. "I won't desire"
is quite the right thing to say, even if "I don't desire"
cannot yet be said by the vital. Still there is something in
the being that can even say "I don't desire" and refuse to
recognise the vital desire as part of the true being. It is
that consciousness which the peace and power bring that
has to be recognised as the true "I" and made permanent
in front.[231]

SRI AUROBINDO

These thoughts that attack in sleep or in the state between
sleep and waking do not belong to any part of your
conscious being, but come either from the subconscient or
from the surrounding atmosphere through the subconscient. If they are thoughts you had in the past and have
thrown out from you, then what rises must be impressions

left by them in the subconscient – for all things thought, felt or experienced leave such impressions which can rise from there in sleep. Or the thoughts can have gone out from you into the environmental consciousness, that is, an atmosphere of consciousness which we carry around us and through which we are connected with universal Nature and from there they may be trying to return upon you. As it is difficult for them to succeed in the waking state, they take advantage of the absence of conscious control in sleep and appear there....

It is to be hoped that as you have rejected them, they will not come again, but if they do, then you must put a conscious will before going to sleep that they should not come. A suggestion of that kind on the subconscient is often successful, if not at once, after a time; for the subconscient learns to obey the will put upon it in the waking state.[232]

SRI AUROBINDO

It would be easier to get rid of wrong movements when you bring down a settled peace and equanimity into that part of the being. There will then be more of an automatic rejection of such movements and less need of *tapasyā*.[233]

SRI AUROBINDO

It is quite normal for difficulties to come back... and it is not a proof that no progress has been made. The recurrence (after one has thought one has conquered) is not unaccountable. I have explained in my writings what happens. When a habitual movement long embedded in the nature is cast out, it takes refuge in some less enlightened part of the nature, and when cast out of the rest of the nature, it takes refuge in the subconscient and from there surges up when you least expect it or comes up in dreams or sudden inconscient movements or it goes out and remains in wait in the environmental being through which the universal Nature works and attacks from there as a force from outside trying to recover its kingdom by a suggestion or repetition of old movements. One has to stand fast till the power of return fades away. These returns or attacks must be regarded not as parts of oneself, but as invasions – and rejected without allowing any depression or discouragement. If the mind does not sanction them, if the vital refuses to welcome them, if the physical remains steady and refuses to obey the physical urge, then the recurrence of the thought, the vital impulse, the physical feeling will begin to lose its last holds and finally they will be too feeble to cause any trouble.[234]

SRI AUROBINDO

If you do not accept certain movements, then naturally, when they find that they can't manifest, gradually they diminish in force and stop occurring. If you refuse to express everything that is of a lower kind, little by little the very thing disappears, and the consciousness is emptied of lower things. It is by refusing to give expression – I mean not only in action but also in thought, in feeling. When impulses, thoughts, emotions come, if you refuse to express them, if you push them aside and remain in a state of inner aspiration and calm, then gradually they lose their force and stop coming. So the consciousness is emptied of its lower movements.

But for instance, when undesirable thoughts come, if you look at them, observe them, if you take pleasure in following them in their movements, they will never stop coming. It is the same thing when you have undesirable feelings or sensations: if you pay attention to them, concentrate on them or even look at them with a certain indulgence, they will never stop. But if you absolutely refuse to receive and express them, after some time they stop. You must be patient and very persistent.

In a great aspiration, if you can put yourself into contact with something higher, some influence of your psychic being or some light from above, and if you can manage to put this in touch with these lower movements, naturally they stop more quickly. But before even being able to draw these things by aspiration, you can already stop those movements from finding expression in you by a very persistent and patient refusal. When thoughts which you do not like come, if you just brush them away and do not pay them any attention at all, after some time they won't come any longer. But you must do this very persistently and regularly.[235]

THE MOTHER

## 9. Possessing Nothing

*Happy indeed are we who own nothing. We shall feed upon delight like the radiant gods.*

The Dhammapada

We could translate it [the verse] like this: "Happy is he

who possesses nothing, he will partake of the delight of the radiant gods." To possess nothing does not at all mean not to make use of anything, not to have anything at one's disposal. "Happy is he who possesses nothing": he is someone who has no sense of possession, who can make use of things when they come to him, knowing that they are not his, that they belong to the Supreme, and who, for the same reason, does not regret it when things leave him; he finds it quite natural that the Lord who gave him these things should take them away from him for others to enjoy. Such a man finds equal joy in the use of things as in the absence of things. When you have them at your disposal, you receive them as a gift of Grace and when they leave you, when they have been taken away from you, you live in the joy of destitution. For it is the sense of ownership that makes you cling to things, makes you their slave, otherwise one could live in constant joy and in the ceaseless movement of things that come and go and pass, that bring with them both the sense of fullness when they are there and, when they go, the delight of detachment.

Delight! Delight means to live in the Truth, to live in communion with Eternity, with the true Life, the Light that never fails. Delight means to be free, free with the true Freedom, the Freedom of the constant, invariable union with the Divine Will.

Gods are those that are immortal, who are not bound to the vicissitudes of material life in all its narrowness, pettiness, unreality and falsehood.

Gods are those who are turned to the Light, who live in the Power and the Knowledge; that is what the Buddha means, he does not mean the gods of religion. They are beings who have the divine nature, who may live in human bodies, but free from ignorance and falsehood.

When you no longer possess anything, you can become as vast as the universe.[236]

THE MOTHER

There should be no attachment – to any object or any mode of life. You must be absolutely free. If you want to have the true yogic attitude, you must be able to accept everything that comes from the Divine and let it go easily and without regret. The attitude of the ascetic who says, "I want nothing" and the attitude of the man of the world who says, "I want this thing" are the same. The one may be as much attached to his renunciation as the other to his possession.[237]

THE MOTHER

It is much more difficult not to be attached to the things you possess than to possess nothing. This is something that has been known for centuries. It requires a much greater quality not to be attached to the things one possesses than to be without any possessions or to reduce one's possessions to a strict minimum. It is much more difficult. It is a much higher degree of moral worth. Simply this attitude: when a thing comes to you, to take it, use it; when for one reason or another it goes away, to let it go and not regret it. Not to refuse it when it comes, to know how to adapt yourself and not to regret it when it goes.[238]

THE MOTHER

## 10. Physical Body – Food

Our first step in this path of knowledge, having once determined in our intellect that what seems is not the Truth, that the self is not the body or life or mind, since these are only its forms, must be to set right our mind in its practical relation with the life and the body so that it may arrive at its own right relation with the Self. This it is easiest to do by a device... it is to create a separation between the Prakriti and the Purusha. The Purusha, the soul that knows and commands has got himself involved in the workings of his executive conscious force, so that he mistakes this physical working of it which we call the body for himself; he forgets his own nature as the soul that knows and commands; he believes his mind and soul to be subject to the law and working of the body; he forgets that he is so much else besides that is greater than the physical form; he forgets that the mind is really greater than Matter and ought not to submit to its obscurations, reactions, habit of inertia, habit of incapacity; he forgets that he is more even than the mind, a Power which can raise the mental being above itself; that he is the Master, the Transcendent and it is not fit the Master should be enslaved to his own workings, the Transcendent imprisoned in a form which exists only as a trifle in its own being. All this forgetfulness has to be cured by the Purusha remembering his own true nature and first by his remembering that the body is only a working and only one working of Prakriti.

We say then to the mind "This is a working of Prakriti, this is neither thyself nor myself; stand back from it." We shall find, if we try, that the mind has this power of detachment and can stand back from the body not only in idea, but in act and as it were physically or rather vitally. This detachment of the mind must be strengthened by a certain attitude of indifference to the things of the body; we must not care essentially about its sleep or its waking, its movement or its rest, its pain or its pleasure, its health or ill-health, its vigour or its fatigue, its comfort or its discomfort, or what it eats or drinks. This does not mean that we shall not keep the body in right order so far as we can; we have not to fall into violent asceticisms or a positive neglect of the physical frame. But we have not either to be affected in mind by hunger or thirst or discomfort or ill-health or attach the importance which the physical and vital man attaches to the things of the body, or indeed any but a quite subordinate and purely instrumental importance. Nor must this instrumental importance be allowed to assume the proportions of a necessity; we must not for instance imagine that the purity of the mind depends on the things we eat or drink, although during a certain stage restrictions in eating and drinking are useful to our inner progress; nor on the other hand must we continue to think that the dependence of the mind or even of the life on food and drink is anything more than a habit, a customary relation which Nature has set up between these principles. As a matter of fact the food we take can be reduced by contrary habit and new relation to a minimum without the mental or vital vigour being in any way reduced; even on the contrary with a judicious development they can be trained to a greater potentiality of vigour by learning to rely on the secret fountains of mental and vital energy with which they are connected more than upon the minor aid of physical ailments. This aspect of self-discipline is however more important in the Yoga of self-perfection than here; for our present purpose the important point is the renunciation by the mind of attachment to or dependence on the things of the body.

Thus disciplined the mind will gradually learn to take up towards the body the true attitude of the Purusha. First of all, it will know the mental Purusha as the upholder of the body and not in any way the body itself; for it is quite other than the physical existence which it upholds by the mind through the agency of the vital force. This will come to be so much the normal attitude of the whole being to the physical frame that the latter will feel to us as if something external and detachable like the dress we wear or an instrument we happen to be carrying in our hand. We may even come to feel that the body is in a certain sense non-existent except as a sort of partial expression of our vital force and of our mentality. These experiences are signs that the mind is coming to a right poise regarding the body, that it is exchanging the false viewpoint of the mentally obsessed and captured by physical sensation for the viewpoint of the true truth of things.

Secondly, with regard to the movements and experiences of the body, the mind will come to know the Purusha seated within it as, first, the witness or observer of the movements and, secondly, the knower or perceiver of the experiences. It will cease to consider in thought or feel in sensation these movements and experiences as its own but rather consider and feel them as not its own, as operations of Nature governed by the qualities of Nature and their interaction upon each other. This detachment can be made so normal and carried so far that there will be a kind of division between the mind and the body and the former will observe and experience the hunger, thirst, pain, fatigue, depression, etc. of the physical being as if they were experiences of some other person with whom it has so close a *rapport* as to be aware of all that is going on within him. This division is a great means, a great step towards mastery; for the mind comes to observe these things first without being overpowered and finally without being at all affected by them, dispassionately, with clear understanding but with perfect detachment. This is the initial liberation of the mental being from servitude to the body; for by right knowledge put steadily into practice liberation comes inevitably.

Finally, the mind will come to know the Purusha in the mind as the master of Nature whose sanction is necessary to her movements. It will find that as the giver of the sanction he can withdraw the original fiat from the previous habits of Nature and that eventually the habit will cease or change in the direction indicated by the will of the Purusha; not at once, for the old sanction persists as an obstinate consequence of the past Karma of Nature until that is exhausted, and a good deal also depends on the force of the habit and the idea of fundamental necessity which the mind had previously attached to it; but if it is not one of the fundamental habits Nature has established for the relation of the mind, life and body and if the old sanction is not renewed by the mind or the habit willingly indulged, then eventually the change will come. Even the habit of hunger and thirst can be minimised, inhibited, put away; the habit of disease can be similarly minimised and gradually eliminated and in the meantime the power of the mind to set right the disorders of the body whether by conscious manipulation of vital force or by simple mental fiat will immensely increase. By a similar process the habit by which the bodily nature associates certain forms and degrees of activity with strain, fatigue, incapacity can be rectified and the power, freedom, swiftness, effectivenes of the work whether physical or mental which can be done with this bodily instrument marvellously increased, doubled, tripled, decupled.[239]

SRI AUROBINDO

It is certainly not very yogic to be so harassed by the importunity of the palate.... In this as in many other matters..., if you want to do yoga, you must take more and more in all matters, small or great, the yogic attitude. In our path that attitude is not one of forceful suppression, but of detachment and equality with regard to the objects of desire. Forceful suppression* stands on the same level as free indulgence; in both cases, the desire remains; in the one it is fed by indulgence, in the other it lies latent and exasperated by suppression. It is only when one stands back, separates oneself from the lower vital, refusing to regard its desires and clamours as one's own, and cultivates an entire equality and equanimity in the consciousness with respect to them that the lower vital itself becomes gradually purified and itself also calm and equal. Each wave of desire as it comes must be observed, as quietly and with as much unmoved detachment as you would observe something going on outside you, and allowed to pass, rejected from the consciousness, and the

---

* Fasting comes under the head; it is of no use for this purpose. Abandon that idea altogether.

true movement, the true consciousness steadily put in its place.[240]

Sri Aurobindo

What is necessary is to take enough food and think no more about it, taking it as a means for the maintenance of the physical instrument only. But just as one should not overeat, so one should not diminish unduly – it produces a reaction which defeats the object – for the object is not to allow either the greed for food or the heavy tamas of the physical which is the result of excessive eating to interfere with the concentration on the spiritual experience and progress. If the body is left insufficiently nourished, it will think of food more than otherwise.[241]

Sri Aurobindo

Perhaps with regard to the greed for food, your attitude has not been quite correct. Greed for food has to be overcome, but it has not to be given too much thought. The proper attitude to food is a certain equality. Food is for the maintenance of the body and one should take enough for that – what the body needs; if one gives less the body feels the need and hankers; if you give more, then that is indulging the vital. As for particular foods the palate likes, the attitude of the mind and vital should be, "If I get, I take; if I don't get, I shall not mind." One should not think too much of food either to indulge or unduly to repress – that is the best.[242]

Sri Aurobindo

Too much eating makes the body material and heavy, eating too little makes it weak and nervous – one has to find the true harmony and balance between the body's need and the food taken.[243]

SRI AUROBINDO

Physically, we depend upon food to live – unfortunately. For with food, we daily and constantly take in a formidable amount of inconscience, of *tamas*, heaviness, stupidity. One can't do otherwise – unless constantly, without a break, we remain completely aware and, as soon as an element is introduced into our body, we immediately work upon it to extract from it only the light and reject all that may darken our consciousness. This is the origin and rational explanation of the religious practice of consecrating one's food to God before taking it. When eating one aspires that this food may not be taken for the little human ego but as an offering to the divine consciousness within oneself. In all yogas, all religions, this is encouraged. This is the origin of that practice, of contacting the consciousness behind, precisely to diminish as much as possible the absorption of an inconscience which increases daily, constantly, without one's being aware of it.[244]

THE MOTHER

All these [giving up indulgence in food, tea, etc.] are external things that have their use, but what I mean [by "the complete attitude of the sadhak"] is something more inward. I mean not to be interested in outward things for their own sake, following after them with desire, but at all times to be intent on one's soul, living centrally in the inner being and its progress, taking outward things and action only as a means for the inner progress.[245]

SRI AUROBINDO

## 11. Progress for the Sake of Progress

... a supreme disinterestedness and a supreme liberation is to follow the discipline of self-perfection, the march of progress, not with a precise end in view..., the liberation of Nirvana, but because this march of progress is the profound law and the purpose of earthly life, the truth of universal existence and because you put yourself in harmony with it, spontaneously, whatever the result may be.

There is a deep trust in the divine Grace, a total surrender to the divine Will, an integral adhesion to the divine Plan which makes one do the thing to be done without concern for the result. That is the perfect liberation.[246]

THE MOTHER

When you begin to advance towards inner and outer perfection, the difficulties start at the same time.

I have very often heard people saying, "Oh! now that I am trying to be good, everybody seems to be bad to me!" But this is precisely to teach you that one should not be good with an interested motive, one should not be good so that others will be good to you – one must be good for the sake of being good.

It is always the same lesson: one must do as well as one can, the best one can, but without expecting a result, without doing it with a view to the result. Just this attitude, to expect a reward for a good action – to become good because one thinks that this will make life easier – takes away all value from the good action.

You must be good for the love of goodness, you must be just for the love of justice, you must be pure for the love of purity and you must be disinterested for the love of disinterestedness; then you are sure to advance on the way.[247]

THE MOTHER

As with everything in yoga, the effort for progress must be made for the love of the effort for progress. The joy of effort, the aspiration for progress must be enough in themselves, quite independent of the result. Everything one does in yoga must be done for the joy of doing it, and not in view of the result one wants to obtain.... Indeed, in life, always, in all things, the result does not belong to us. And if we want to keep the right attitude, we must act, feel, think, strive spontaneously, for *that* is what we must do, and not in view of the result to be obtained.

As soon as we think of the result we begin to bargain and that takes away all sincerity from the effort. You make an effort to progress because you feel within you the need, the *imperative* need to make an effort and progress; and this effort is the gift you offer to the Divine Consciousness in you, the Divine Consciousness in the Universe, it is your way of expressing your gratitude, offering your self; and whether this results in progress or not is of no importance. You will progress when it is decided that the time has come to progress and not because you desire it.

If you wish to progress, if you make an effort to control yourself for instance, to overcome certain defects, weaknesses, imperfections, and if you expect to get a more or less immediate result from your effort, your effort loses all sincerity, it becomes a bargaining. You say, "See! I am going to make an effort, but that's because I want this in exchange for my effort". You are no longer spontaneous, no longer natural.[248]

THE MOTHER

> *As the elephant on the battlefield endures the arrow*
> *shot from the bow, so also shall I patiently bear*
> *insult, for truly there are many of evil mind in the*
> *world.*
>
> The Dhammapada

The... verse gives some very wise advice: the war elephant who has been well trained does not start running away as soon as he receives an arrow. He continues to advance and bears the pain, with no change in his attitude of heroic resistance. Those who wish to follow the true path will naturally be exposed to the attacks of all forms of bad will, which not only do not understand, but generally hate what they do not understand.

If you are worried, grieved or even discouraged by the malicious stupidities that men say about you, you will not advance far on the way. And such things come to you, not because you are unlucky or because your lot is not a happy one, but because, on the contrary, the divine Consciousness and the divine Grace take your resolution seriously and allow the circumstances to become a touchstone on your way, to see whether your resolution is sincere and whether you are strong enough to face the difficulties.

Therefore, if anyone sneers at you or says something that is not very charitable, the first thing you should do is to look within yourself for whatever weakness or imperfection has allowed such a thing to happen and not to be disconsolate, indignant or aggrieved, because people do not apppreciate you at what you think to be your true value; on the contrary, you must be thankful to the divine Grace for having pointed out to you the weakness or imperfection or deformation that you must correct.

Therefore, instead of being unhappy, you can be fully satisfied and derive advantage, a great advantage from the harm that was intended against you.

Besides, if you truly want to follow the path and practise yoga, you must not do it for appreciation or honour, you must do it because it is an imperative need of your being, because you cannot be happy in any other way. Whether people appreciate you or do not appreciate you, it is of absolutely no importance. You may tell yourself beforehand that the further you are from ordinary men, foreign to the ordinary mode of being, the less people will appreciate you, quite naturally, because they will not understand you. And I repeat, it has absolutely no importance.

True sincerity consists in advancing on the way because you cannot do otherwise, to consecrate yourself to the divine life because you cannot do otherwise, to seek to transform your being and come out into the light because you cannot do otherwise, because it is the purpose of your life.

When it is like that you may be sure that you are on the right path.[249]

THE MOTHER

# GLOSSARY OF TERMS AND NAMES

*abhyāsa* — constant practice (of a disciplinary method).

*agni* (Agni) — fire; the godhead of fire.

*ānanda* (Ananda) — bliss, delight, beatitude, spiritual ecstasy; a self-delight which is the very nature of the transcendent and infinite existence.

*anirviṇṇacetasā* — with a consciousness free from despondency.

**Anumanta** — giver of sanction.

**Aspiration** — the yearning of the being for higher things, for the Divine, for all that belongs to the higher or divine consciousness.

**Being** — the Self; the sole and fundamental Reality or Truth of existence; all that exists is part of the one indivisible Being.

The One Being manifests itself on different planes or levels of consciousness, and in the individual being is constituted by different distinguishable parts of the indivisible Being.

The part of our nature of which we are normally conscious is our surface or outer being, consisting of the body, the (surface) vital (related to life-energy, instincts, desires, emotions, etc.) and the (surface) mind (having to do with cognition, intelligence, ideas, thought perceptions, etc.).

Behind this superficial consciousness there exists a far greater, deeper and more powerful consciousness in touch with the universal planes of Mind, Life and Matter. This hidden consciousness, referred to as our inner or true being, consists of the true or inner mental, the true or inner vital and the true or inner physical, with the psychic (the soul) as the innermost being, which supports all the different parts in the manifestation.

The inner being is also sometimes referred to as the subliminal (being). It opens above to the superconscient and below to the subconscient and the inconscient.

*bhakti* (Bhakti) — devotion; love for the Divine.

**Brahman** — the Reality; the Absolute; the Spirit; the Supreme

Being; the One besides whom there is nothing else existent.

**Consciousness** — the self-aware force of existence whose energy and movement create the universe and all that is in it; consciousness is usually identified with mind, but mental consciousness is only one gradation of consciousness, there being gradations of consciousness both above and below mental consciousness; *see also* **Being**.

**Detachment** — The state of non-attachment resulting from the conquest of egoistic desire, likes and dislikes.

**Dhammapada, the** — a Buddhist scripture containing the teachings of the Buddha.

**Dharma** — Law; the deepest law of one's nature; literally, that which one lays hold of and which holds things together.

**Divine, the** — the Supreme Being from whom all comes and in whom all lives. In its supreme Truth the Divine is absolute and infinite peace, consciousness, existence, power and delight. The Transcendent, the Cosmic (Universal) and the Individual are three powers of the Divine, underlying the whole of manifestation.

**Equality** — equal-mindedness; *see also* **samatā**.

**Gita, the** — short form of Bhagavad Gita, "the Song of the Blessed Lord"; a celebrated scripture in the form of a dialogue between Lord Krishna and Arjuna in an episode in the Mahabharata.

**Grace, the (Divine Grace)** — higher Divine Force other than the force of Karma which comes down to help an aspirant.

**Guru** — spiritual teacher or guide.

**Ignorance, the** — the consciousness of Multiplicity as distinguished from the Knowledge, the consciousness of Unity; a view of the reality based on separative or egoistic consciousness.

**Inconscience (the Inconscient)** — the most involved state of Being; all the evolved powers of the Being – Matter, Life, Mind – have emerged successively out of the Inconscient; *see also* **Being**.

**Inner Being** — *see* **Being**.

**Karma** — action, work; the chain of act and consequence.

**Karmayoga** — the spiritual path based on works.

**Mantra** — words having a spiritual power; sacred syllable, name or mystic formula generally used for repetition.

**Mara** — in Buddhism: the Destroyer, the Evil One, who tempts man to indulge his passions; conscious devil or self-existent principle of evil.

**Mind (the mental)** — the part of the being which has to do with thinking and intelligence; *see also* **Being**.

**Mother, the** — the Divine in its aspect of Consciousness Force; the Divine Conscious Force that dominates all existence and upholds the universe.

**Outer being** — *see* **Being**.

**Prakriti (*prakṛti*)** — Nature; outer being composed of the outer physical, outer vital and outer mental.

*prārabdha karma* — mechanical action of Prakriti continuing by force of old impulsion and past habit and action.

**Psychic Being** — the individual soul; when the psyche, the soul-principle present in all life and matter, begins to develop an individuality in the course of evolution, that psychic individuality is called the psychic being; *see also* **Being**.

**Purusha (*puruṣa*)** — Conscious Being; conscious Soul; essential being supporting the play of Prakriti; the Purusha represents the true being on whatever plane it manifests – physical, vital, mental, psychic.

**Rajasic** — dominantly characterised by *rajas*, the quality of passion or drive of propensity; impelled by desire and instinct.

**Rakshasa** — giant; power of darkness, a [hostile] being of the vital plane.

**Ramakrishna** — Sri Ramakrishna Paramahansa (1836-86), one of the foremost spiritual teachers of modern India.

**Realisation** — attainment of a spiritual goal; when an inner experience, such as that of spiritual Peace, Light, Force,

Love, Bliss, the Divine Presence, etc. becomes very positive or frequent or continuous or part of one's normal state of consciousness – instead of coming only in flashes, snatches or rare visitations – it is spoken of as a realisation.

**Rejection** — the inner refusal of movements (thoughts, feelings and actions) which are contrary to one's higher aspirations.

**Rishi** — seer; sage.

**Sadhak** — one who practises a spiritual discipline.

**Sadhana** — the practice of a spiritual discipline.

*samatā* — equal-mindedness to all things and happenings; equanimity under all conditions.

**Sattwic** — dominantly characterised by *sattwa*, the quality of poise, peace, harmony, purity and knowledge.

**Self, the** — the original and essential nature of our existence; *see also* **Being**.

**Siddhi** — perfection; success, attainment of the goals of yoga.

**Subconscient** — the part of the being which is below the physical consciousness, close to the Inconscient; it meets the Inconscient and in it the Inconscient struggles into a half-consciousness; *see also* **Being**.

**Surface consciousness** — *see* **Being**.

*svabhāva* — one's own essential or inborn temperament, nature or character.

**Tamasic** — dominantly characterised by *tamas*, the quality of inertia, ignorance, incapacity and inaction.

**Tapaswi** — one who practises Tapasya.

**Tapasya (*tapasyā*)** — effort, energy or austerity of the personal will for self-control or self-transformation.

**Titanic** — of the nature of a Titan (hostile being of the vital plane).

**Transformation** — a radical change of consciousness, by the bringing down of the higher, divine consciousness and nature into the lower nature of mind, life and body, and the replacement of the lower by the higher.

**Vairagya (*vairāgya*)** — disgust with the world; complete cessation of desire and attachment.

**Vital, the** — the life-nature of the being, made up of life-energy, sensations, instincts, impulses, feelings and desires; *see also* Being.

**Vivekananda, Swami** — monastic name of Narendranath Dutta (1863-1902), the most famous disciple of Sri Ramakrishna and one of the great spiritual teachers of modern India.

**Yoga** — "joining", union; the discipline by which one seeks consciously and deliberately to realise the Divine or, more generally, to attain a higher consciousness.

*yogin* (Yogi) — one who practises yoga; one who is established in spiritual realisation.

# REFERENCES

The extracts in this compilation are contained in the following publications of Sri Aurobindo Ashram, Pondicherry, India:

SA = Sri Aurobindo Birth Centenary Library
MO = Collected Works of the Mother – Centenary Edition

The first number after SA or MO indicates the number of the volume in the series. The number following it indicates the page number.

The titles of the volumes from which the references have been drawn are as follows:

## SRI AUROBINDO BIRTH CENTENARY LIBRARY

## COLLECTED WORKS OF THE MOTHER

1. MO 3:154-55
2. MO 6:123-24
3. MO 10:247
4. SA 24:1696
5. SA 23:579-80
6. MO 9:29-31
7. MO 6:340-41
8. MO 5:202-03
9. MO 6:154
10. MO 3:279
11. MO 3:203-06
12. MO 8:289-91
13. SA 24:1403
14. MO 14:234
15. SA 24:1698
16. SA 23:550
17. SA 23:550
18. MO 6:176-77
19. SA 24:1627-28
20. MO 8:257-58
21. MO 10:58-59
22. SA 23:597
23. MO 14:249
24. MO 14:249
25. MO 14:250
26. SA 23:629
27. SA 24:1709
28. MO 1:105
29. MO 1:26
30. MO 1:96
31. MO 1:102
32. MO 3:220-21
33. SA 24:1392
34. SA 23:706-07
35. SA 24:1684
36. SA 24:1687
37. SA 24:1684-85
38. SA 24:1392
39. MO 6:350
40. SA 23:826
41. SA 23:826
42. SA 23:826
43. SA 23:826
44. SA 24:1684
45. SA 23:826
46. SA 23:823
47. SA 23:823-24
48. MO 3:292
49. SA 23:553
50. SA 23:665-66
51. SA 23:709
52. SA 23:709-10
53. SA 23:710
54. SA 23:711
55. SA 24:1640
56. MO 10:75-77
57. MO 5:303-04
58. MO 9:417
59. SA 22:151
60. SA 23:583
61. SA 23:691-92
62. SA 23:692
63. SA 23:678
64. SA 25:272-73
65. MO 2:49-51
66. SA 23:671
67. SA 23:531
68. SA 23:516
69. SA 23:678
70. SA 23:679
71. SA 23:852
72. SA 23:680-81
73. SA 23:677
74. SA 23:677
75. SA 23:669
76. SA 23:678

77. SA 23:674
78. SA 23:701
79. SA 23:701
80. SA 23:705
81. MO 4:156
82. SA 23:719
83. SA 23:717
84. SA 23:717
85. SA 23:717
86. SA 24:1686
87. SA 24:1640
88. SA 24:1624
89. MO 14:234-35
90. MO 14:235
91. MO 14:235
92. MO 17:406
93. MO 6:242
94. MO 14:248
95. MO 14:236
96. MO 14:236
97. MO 14:236
98. SA 24:1708
99. MO 5:213-15
100. MO 6:343-44
101. MO 6:242-43
102. MO 6:262-64
103. MO 4:169-70
104. MO 4:72-74
105. MO 3:215
106. SA 24:1756
107. MO 3:33-34
108. MO 3:35
109. SA 24:1615
110. SA 23:583
111. MO 7:10-11
112. SA 24:1710
113. SA 24:1710
114. SA 24:1345

115. SA 23:541
116. SA 24:1425
117. SA 24:1698
118. MO 14:234
119. MO 14:239
120. MO 14:239
121. MO 14:239
122. MO 7:396-97
123. MO 3:256-57
124. SA 24:1688-89
125. MO 9:423-24
126. SA 23:570-71
127. SA 23:569
128. SA 23:570
129. SA 24:1672-73
130. SA 24:1572
131. SA 24:1567
132. SA 24:1567
133. SA 24:1569
134. SA 24:1563
135. SA 24:1580
136. SA 24:1580
137. SA 24:1580
138. SA 24:1580
139. SA 24:1580
140. SA 24:1636
141. SA 24:1636
142. MO 10:268
143. SA 24:1686
144. SA 23:565
145. SA 23:552
146. SA 23:567
147. SA 23:567
148. SA 23:568
149. SA 23:568
150. SA 23:555
151. SA 23:651
152. SA 23:651

153. SA 23:651
154. SA 23:654
155. SA 23:560
156. SA 23:560
157. SA 23:560-61
158. SA 23:561
159. MO 3:190
160. MO 6:132-33
161. SA 23:562-63
162. MO 3:8-9
163. MO 3:192-93
164. SA 23:591
165. SA 23:591-92
166. SA 23:592
167. SA 23:611
168. SA 23:593
169. SA 23:593
170. SA 23:593-94
171. MO 3:189
172. MO 14:85
173. MO 14:85
174. MO 14:85
175. MO 14:85
176. MO 14:85
177. SA 23:573
178. SA 23:575-76
179. SA 23:577-78
180. SA 23:579
181. SA 23:581
182. SA 23:584
183. SA 23:584
184. SA 23:584-85
185. SA 23:585
186. SA 23:585
187. SA 23:585
188. SA 23:587-88
189. SA 23:549
190. MO 6:122-23

191. SA 23:624
192. MO 4:251
193. SA 23:552
194. SA 23:623
195. SA 23:623
196. SA 23:629
197. SA 23:629
198. SA 23:629
199. MO 8:41-42
200. MO 3:136
201. SA 24:1358-59
202. SA 24:1635
203. SA 24:1365
204. SA 24:1359
205. MO 3:139
206. MO 8:23
207. MO 14:189
208. MO 14:189
209. MO 14:189-90
210. MO 14:190
211. MO 3:2
212. MO 4:341-42
213. MO 3:202-03
214. SA 24:1711
215. SA 24:1711
216. SA 23:1002
217. SA 23:1006
218. SA 23:1006
219. SA 23:1006-07
220. MO 8:398
221. SA 23:1008-09
222. SA 23:1012
223. SA 22:125
224. SA 22:125-26
225. SA 24:1398-99
226. SA 24:1401-02
227. SA 24:1402
228. SA 24:1402

229. SA 24:1402-03
230. SA 24:1403
231. SA 24:1403
232. SA 24:1602-03
233. SA 24:1683
234. SA 24:1712-13
235. MO 6:329-30
236. MO 3:252-54
237. MO 3:9
238. MO 6:429
239. SA 20:328-31

240. SA 24:1465-66
241. SA 24:1466
242. SA 24:1466-67
243. SA 24:1467
244. MO 4:334-35
245. SA 23:888-89
246. MO 3:298
247. MO 3:264-65
248. MO 9:316-17
249. MO 3:281-84

# INDEX